Attributes of the Moth

Marylinn
Kelly

Karen Mireau Books
Sonoma | California

ISBN: 978-1-968822-07-1

Front & Back Cover Art:
The Energy Is Taken
Then Reappears In Other Forms
by Mike Leadabrand.

Front & Back Photos
by Tom Oldfield.

Dedicated to:

Claire Beynon, Karen Mireau, and Penelope Todd for their generous hearts and belief in my work, without whom this book would not exist.

Contents

Part II

Part III

Part IV

Part V

Part VI

Part VII

Introduction

The special volume you now hold in your hands is a testament to love, friendship, art and literature. As is often the case in things that are of true worth, it began as a series of gifts.

First, there was the gift of the many years of blog posts frequently titled "Word of the Week" that author and artist Marylinn Kelly crafted and posted in Blogger from 2008 to 2018. Some have been shared on FaceBook.

Then, there was the inspired notion by Marylinn's dear friends Claire Beynon and Penelope Todd to gather many of Marylinn's blog writings in book form.

Yet another gracious and unexpected gift came from Marylinn's brother, Mike Leadabrand, who created the special original oil painting that graces both the front and back covers.

It then became my turn, as publisher, to assemble all of these gifts in one place.

I believe I can speak for all of the contributors that it has been an ongoing occasion of great joy to work on this book, and that it has been a collaboration that exceeded any expectation.

In the process, I received yet another beautiful gift—that of working with Marylinn, whom I've known now for over forty years. And, I made two new delightful friends in Claire and Penelope, both of whom are highly creative artists, writers, and publishers in their own right.

In *Attributes of the Moth,* Marylinn offers us words conjured from daily life, but whose definitions quickly transcend the ordinary.

Turn to any page. Her musings on art, life, love, loss, and human frailty speak to the soul center that resides in each of us, becoming an oceanic sort of oracle—one that is well worth exploring—and sharing with those you love.

Happiness & Inspiration,
— Karen Mireau
Karen Mireau Books

Preface

By now, some of my secrets have been pulled from under the couch cushions and put on the table. Among these are the revelation that I find life to be teeming, jumping with symbolism, that I willingly allow a representative portion of something to stand in for the still-to-come whole, that metaphor is my native language and very little is only what it seems.

In a short, perhaps five-minute segment of a recent podcast, there was a meditative exercise in which listeners were directed to find a spirit guide. The practitioner spoke of eagles, for the ability to fly would be required of the guide. Mine arrived. It was a moth.

It may be my most basic belief that we are here—wherever we are geographically, emotionally, physically in this moment—to be of assistance to each other. Assistance, in this case, can mean anything. Without rushing to Google, I thought of the moth, an extreme example of transformation, starting life as one form and becoming a different creature. I am not who I used to be. Teachers, awareness and opportunities continue to find me, carrying me out of dimness, discouragement, into a brighter land. Mulling and pondering—and daydreaming—are natural states, taking the measure of a situation, mostly by intuition, interpreting, perceiving, feeling. Feeling my way toward knowledge, insight, information.

When I looked into what moth brings as a totem I found: the ability to perceive with clarity, strong healing abilities, protection for traveling between darkness and the light, finding light in darkness, metamorphosis and, in common with the phoenix, rising from the ashes, in moth's case of the flames to which it is drawn. What better sidekick?

The title—*Attributes of the Moth*—is one of those, "Quick, write this down," flashes. Forgive me, please, if I repeat myself. Life as I have come to know it is fraught with meaning—likely it always was, but I had no skills. These, too, are days of myth and fable, truths revealed in waking, walking dreams. No wonder fiction explores parallel universes, wormholes, wrinkles in time. How else to explain being conscious of treading the ordinary path of oil changes, bill paying, medical procedures, clothes that need washing or detecting an unpleasant odor in the refrigerator and, in the same moments, seeing the story within the story, the plan behind the random event, the bigger picture?

For some of you, this might be like my talking in tongues. That may be a fair comparison. The best we can hope for is to know our own truths and to allow others to know theirs. If we share common ground, there is much to discuss. Meanwhile, I may be found in a somewhat unkempt state wearing soft clothes that feel like pajamas, looking at the sky from my second-floor window with a never-abandoned wish to have the ability to fly.

Some of these essays contain reference to music, art and assorted visuals which were part of the blog posts. I've tried to delete misleading references but names of people and of works remain. If unknown to you, I invite you to look them up.

Also, the essays are not in chronological order, so seasons, if mentioned, may skip around. They are grouped according to the vision of those who compiled the book, for which I am grateful.

In the process of writing the 951 blog posts that exist, I became part of a community of fellow seekers who found a blog to be the perfect home for their thoughts and creativity. It came to me to see us as a band, far-flung and disparate but following the same star.

"Just say you're with the band," became a notion that fit us all.

— Marylinn Kelly
South Pasadena, California, 2025

Part I

To teach imagination is to teach everything

Even Einstein told us that imagination is more important than knowledge. How do we know where one begins, leaving the other to follow? I know as well as I know anything that without imagination we might still be cave-dwellers or fishermen terrified of the Earth's flatness. In a not very original comparison, imagination feels like flinging open the school doors and letting everyone run free, trusting they will find their place, acquire the information they need to reach their destination, realize there are no walls and no limits.

To dream BIG is an adventure. If the lands we seek are only in our minds, what of it? The realms of Tolkien or Baum or Bradbury may not exist on any maps, still they are as real to us as the corner drugstore in our hometown, much more real than what we may have had presented to us as the system's version of history—pick an era. If our brains were skyscrapers, imagination would be housed on the top floor. Not difficult to reach—there are express elevators—but easily missed because gravity or the status quo or someone's expectations or fears kept us from venturing that far from what we thought we knew.

Mary Chapin Carpenter has a song called *Heroes and Heroines*, in which she tells of risk-takers, people who are unfamiliar with the word impossible, and speaks of our American pioneers, choosing ". . . a life that's never safe and dry . . ." and I found those words resonated for me as epitomizing reasons why we may wish to stay uninformed, unenlightened. Imagination carries the possibility of risk and reward. Yet staying put has never been a guarantee of that safe, dry life, for I don't believe it exists. Fiction has given us examples that appear in everyday language, like falling down the rabbit hole, finding the entrance to Narnia or the road to Oz. Rod Serling's introduction to *Twilight Zone* episodes mentions imagination, in almost the same breath as he speaks of worlds that are ". . . as vast as space and as timeless as infinity."

Two of the three children in our family had imaginary friends and the third sibling lived a vicarious life through a sizable stuffed bear who had a flourishing literary career. I spent years writing dialogue in my head and wondering why, when the people around me spoke, they never used the words I'd prepared for them. Our parents followed creative paths, yet were not wildly outside any norms for their time. I no longer believe in ordinary as an inevitable state; I believe we each possess the capacity for the exceptional. One may choose ordinary but I don't think anyone who wishes to escape can really be stopped. In our minds we discover there are no limits, no walls too high, no thorn hedges too impenetrable, no world which could not exist if we gave it breath and light.

Dream huge. Stare out the window and let your thoughts run everywhere. Let the dam burst, the gargoyles take flight and twin suns rise in the morning. We are so much more than we know, unfettered, unhampered by time. We are the stories and the tellers, we are enormous, we are endless, heart-breakingly beautiful, fierce and wise. We will never be small again.

No small blessings

Venturing into the studio this morning, I was hunting brushes—specifically a set I thought I had seen while burrowing for paint the other day. If one had patience and infinite humor about everything, the puzzle which is the studio could possibly seem amusing. I moved the Christmas tree into the only quadrant of open floor, then rolled a set of drawers into its space, then rearranged objects only slightly smaller to, at last, scoot myself into a spot from which my hands could reach bookshelves and the counter where I KNEW the pastels had once rested.

The brushes were where I expected to find them, so I declared the morning a success. Oh, but there was so much more to come and, in the way of pulling on a sweater against a draft, I was immediately warmed by the not forgotten but unremembered—and vastly useful—material I encountered.

Being human, I have moments during which I fail to count ALL my blessings. I grow amnesiac about the wealth of reference volumes in our books-in-almost-every-room world. Starting in the early '70s, I built a collection of Dover Pictorial Archive titles—copyright-free illustrations collated into volumes by category, such as *Borders, Frames and Decorative Motifs from the 1862 Derriey Typographic Catalog* or *Victorian Fashion.* I have used them in my work, in my volunteer newsletter editing, in projects for fun. Several years ago, I was one of a group of artists asked to donate a copy of a favorite, art-inspiring book for a fund-raising drawing. My offerings were from Dover's clip-art series.

All this studio exploration is in preparation for being half of a team scheduled to do a demonstration on journal pages. I have been revisiting experts (real experts) who give examples and advice on their methods, as it has been a while since I produced any work that fits this description. And on the Dover shelves I found copyable words and buildings, borders and animals, faces and hands and automobiles to include as collage elements on the pages. I realized I had truly lost track of the breadth of subjects in my possession.

The unearthing of each new title added to my sense of uncalculated abundance. While I have been known to do a mental scan of supplies and see the gaps rather than the plenty, there was no way I could escape admitting it today: I am rich in resources.

It is a day of jubilee when we can look at all that surrounds us and see with new eyes. While I knew that useful bits would appear as I foraged, I was unprepared for the gratitude I felt for stumbling into my own life and discovering that, not only was the cupboard not bare, it was brimming. I felt wise that I had built such a useful collection, getting value from it many times over in the past yet having an enhanced awareness of its meaning today. I felt glad that a veil of forgetfulness had kept these treasures from consciousness, so that I also had the pleasure of happy surprise. In addition to the Pictorial Archive library, I found vintage ledgers sent to me by my sister, a keen-eyed antique picker, and a collection of Victorian scrap which had been a friend's gift.

There was a day, during some especially lean times, when I found $20 in a seldom-used purse and felt we had won the lottery—I knew it symbolized the prosperity which surrounds us. If I gave all my moments the attention they deserve, I would likely find that I always have the numbers lined up for a Bingo prize. Today I had the sense that another length of the curtain had been drawn back, a reminder that what I, what we, seek is there, within reach. Waiting for good times turns our gaze in the wrong direction. Yes, things can always get better—and they do—yet right now is clamoring for our attention. My own Oz, a magical place where dreams manifest, hiding behind the Christmas tree, and all I had to do was look.

Lepidoptera

What the order of insects that includes moths and butterflies offers is the ultimate model for transformation. The process of evolving from crawling to entering soupy suspended animation to emerging with wings reminds me—as do attentive friends who remember what I often forget—about process.

Not all aspects of process may look or feel attractive, appealing. If one was always just dandy, it wouldn't be process. Redemption and transformation are two favorite themes, experiences that I believe may be ours but that we achieve not by coming at them head-on but by either tripping over or backing into them, possibly while asleep or in any one of a number of altered states. I feel both are the product of grace, pure grace and not determination.

As I examine my self-proclaimed or self-suspected slackerish leanings I know that grace alone will deliver me. So I look to the lepidoptera and an observable arc of changing from this into that, as aware as I am able to be that my metamorphosis is a lifetime's journey. Ebenezer Scrooge may have received a miraculous overnight awakening. A transition which takes longer is no less welcome, no less a miracle.

Habitat

The magic of place. Theirs, ours.

A postcard from Cuba of Hemingway's desk. Assorted views of Edward Gorey's home on Cape Cod, the not-quite teetering stacks of books, the objects. Stuffed toys in The Alcove. One's natural environment. Our part-Airedale, Heidi, dug herself a cool, snug nest beneath the oleanders and wallowed until she could raise a cloud of dirt in a snowstorm. Then she'd come inside, eat whatever meal my mother had fixed for herself and lie on her bed, hogging the pillow. In the Heidi museum, all aspects of her personality would be recreated by her habitat.

We are comforted by whatever holds us in place. In a favorite movie, *Laura*, Clifton Webb's character says without Laura, he would run amok. So would we all, minus piles, bed covers, trinkets, talismans, the arrangement of pens in a specific box, the exact notebook within arm's reach. I am happy to know there is a ruler or, in a pinch, a tape measure in almost every room. You never know when the size of an A7 envelope will be the most important thing on the agenda. There are scissors in every room that I frequent. There is southern light, a luxury we missed for too long, and a view of tree tops and sky. Drawers of paper, ribbons, clear boxes of rubber stamps.

My newest favorite thing is the "down alternative" comforter I began using in December. There was too much piled on the bed to enjoy it before that. I am not sure how other people, allegedly grown-ups as I may be, create a space that approximates Heidi's trench. I know the books standing and piled to my left beneath the window have a heartbeat. They give off warmth, pulse and speak. In moments of depletion they seem to rally round. Whether I consult them or not, I know they offer wisdom, perspective, safety, an identifiable version of sanity. They are part of my blanket fort, the quilt draped over the card table on a rainy day, pillows encased in cotton washed a million times, softened and faint of hue, familiar and dependable as a grandmother's hug. This is home.

Griot

Pronounced *gree-oh*, I met the word in a review of poet Tim Seibles' collection *Hurdy-Gurdy* last week. I'm not sure I had ever read or heard it before. Defined as "any of a class of musician-entertainers of western Africa whose performances include tribal histories and genealogies; *broadly:* storyteller."

This is the quote in which it appeared:

> *Listening to Tim Seibles sing the poems in this sizzling collection is like listening to the voice of the griot praising, admonishing, cursing, blessing, and calling us together. . . . As a reader of poetry, I appreciated his exquisite crafting and cool, streetwise lyricism. And as a somewhat envious fellow poet, I wished that every rich, textured stanza were mine.*
>
> — Patricia Smith

I imagine you can understand why I needed to make the acquaintance of griot. It was one of those words that bumped into me like a pickpocket at the carnival in another age, helping me to my feet, brushing the sawdust from my sleeve, looking me in the eye. It is a word that makes me happy it exists, that there is a specific name for such a group, such a person. It overflows the banks of storyteller and meanders in all directions.

There are names and phrases by which we might choose to be identified, collections of words that paint who we believe or know ourselves to be, definitions of all to which we aspire. Twenty years ago, two friends and I met on Saturday mornings and worked through Julia Cameron's *The Artist's Way* until we each arrived at a seemingly unreachable destination. For me it involved having a rubber stamp made of my name with the word artist on the line beneath. In the same chamber of imagination where I once pictured my foot fitting into the faux glass slipper that held the Cinderella wristwatch, I will now dream of the California girl who somehow grew, morphed, blossomed and expanded into being likened to a griot. Any of us who seek to bend and tame language, even for a moment, to our will could share the longing.

Unmatched

> *I stood willingly and gladly in the characters of everything - other people, trees, clouds. And this is what I learned, that the world's otherness is antidote to confusion—that standing within this otherness—the beauty and the mystery of the world, out in the fields or deep inside books—can re-dignify the worst-stung heart.*
>
> — Mary Oliver

For me it was occasionally socks of two almost matching colors, there ***is*** more than one shade of brown, or the skirt and sweater in differing, incompatible shades of blue, or so Sandy Lansdale told me in the 7th grade. She didn't use the word *outré* which would have been my mother's choice but her vehemence kept me from ever again wearing those two garments together. Thinking then of unmatched, it never suggested without peer, special, rare, stand-alone. In sets of paper dolls, girlfriends who looked to be the same age but not related each came with a plaid dress. As I mentally wrote the dialogue for their imaginary conversations, they once agreed that all would wear a plaid dress to school on the same day. They viewed this as a unifying statement, proof of a superior sameness. They stood in for the real girls, born around 1944 or 1945 who owned at least two plaid dresses each, replaced when outgrown but often kept as the hem and waistline crept up and up until perhaps the fourth grade when, for me, clothing from the children's department no longer fit.

Even in my Brownie or Scout uniform, I felt the moved-off-to-the-side separation of the overbaked Cheerio or ill-formed animal cracker. The cheese stands alone. I suspect it is the rare child who finds true, deep comfort in being the only one to see how much Aunt Dorothea resembles the actress on the magazine cover when everyone tells her, in so many words, that she's crazy, there is nothing the same about them. An ability to see or know beyond is not welcomed in most families. Time and its grace change that, replacing isolation with attachment to what is unmatched or unequaled within its own sphere. There is such majesty in being the only one of us that will ever exist, a singleton, not relegated to the small table near the door to the kitchen but a presence, embodiment of grandeur, beaming with unique yet universal light without which the world, the galaxy would be too dim and cold to bear.

Palimpsest

A simplification of the noun's meaning is: a manuscript (usually written on papyrus or parchment) on which more than one text has been written with the earlier writing incompletely erased and still visible. The word speaks to me of a more personal rewriting, of how the people we used to be bleed through the strata of time, how the scrims that occlude our past selves are thinner, more revealing in some spots than others, how remnants of our histories allow us to reinterpret the parts we can decipher.

My ruminant tendencies are heightened in the middle of some nights. They may be prompted by dreams or, more likely, result from a sudden awakening that leaves me vulnerable to previously unrealized possibilities. I have sanded and scraped away bits of 28 years in two marriages, the first begun when I was 18, and even through gesso and acrylic washes, decades of becoming, I find those younger selves waiting, looking to me for enlightenment. In a palimpsest, what had been recorded is not quite here, not quite gone. I observe with eyes either more knowing or more kind. The boys/men benefit from these gauzy revisits, as though some of what has been eroded is a hardness of heart in response to pain. There is greater forgiveness for all that I could not have known, appreciation for being not only still here, but softened rather than steeled. Blame and fault grow more faint on the page. Where the words can't be decoded, they appear as dots and blotches. Love's great speckled egg.

A gift? Are you sure? It doesn't look like one

Today's unanswerable question: will we always know the gift when we meet it?

The thought that landed on me as I left an art project in the glue-drying stage was this: what if all that we feel is most shameful, unacceptable, unwelcome, self-destructive and just *ewwwwwww* about ourselves is THE thing that somehow managed to keep us here so that we could grow into the people we were meant to become, people who have more than a vague sense why we are here? Yes, I think and talk to myself in rambling, run-on sentences.

Some of us, and I count myself among them/us, once found human existence more than we thought we could bear. Depression was diagnosed but inefficiently treated and its poisonous swamp gas continued to swirl for years, decades, adding to the sense of despair and, mostly, of having done everything wrong. Apathy and addictions do not enhance self-esteem. One addiction, even two or three, faced down and surrendered still leaves the bunkhouse crowded with shifty layabouts. Will I ever meet a shortbread cookie I don't like? At least for me a combination of flattening medications and advancing age have kept me from continuing to take up with men with whom I, perhaps, ought not to have taken up. But here is what I ponder. What if the cookies and other foodstuffs that do not promote optimal health and what if the drama and sometimes danger of unsuitable companions blunted the pain just enough to make it possible to go on when without them I wouldn't still be here? That could be true, couldn't it? What if those sources of seemingly enduring shame were actually gifts, temporary life preservers, not intended to be used forever but only until no longer needed?

I feel that I'm approaching a crossroads, or maybe it is a summit, after which I and my path will no longer look the same. I have been coming to it, at it, for some time, in the growing company of writing and art and love. There is so much I want to do, so much about what I do that fills me with awe at my good fortune. And that's with various, let us call them limitations. I can imagine what all this would be like with restored or at least enhanced strength, vitality, agility and options. I absolutely believe, whatever IT is, it takes as long as it takes. A great benevolent hand has gotten me this far. How much easier its job if it didn't have to carry quite as much of me, if I could get back to something more identifiable as self-propulsion.

To see shortcomings not as failures but as training wheels, part of the process of becoming, necessary until they're not, what a revelation that would be. I am still, in a way, thinking out loud in answer to my question. I feel there is truth in it, not just an easy out for not yet having become entirely moderate and sensible and consistent. I may never be all of those at the same time or I may. I didn't believe I could do many of the things that are now part of me. Yes, I expect miracles. I have experienced too many to stop now.

Words

Today's author of *Poem-A-Day* is Gregory Orr, who said,

> *When I write a poem, I process experience. I take what's inside me—the raw, chaotic material of feeling or memory—and translate it into words and then shape those words into the rhythmical language we call a poem. This process brings me a kind of wild joy. Before I was powerless and passive in the face of my confusion, but now I am active: the powerful shaper of my experience. I am transforming it into a lucid meaning.*

Those of us who are not poets still face the task of wrestling, shoveling, wrangling and subduing words to do as we would have them do, to speak our truths. Recent experiences with upgrading land lines and internet connections made me acutely aware of being precise about the questions I asked, about verifying what I had been told and then, when bits went awry, of explaining the situation unambiguously to the next representative.

Caring about words can be burdensome. When only THE word will do, not finding it in the memory bank causes distress. Second-best is not good enough in wordville. As a girl, my mother had taken elocution lessons. In those days it seemed to matter more than it currently does whether or not one could speak clearly and confidently. As a result, my sister and I grew up following her patterns of speech. Many a caller on the other end of the phone could not tell one of us from another. It was once pointed out to me that I leave spaces around my words. Yes, I do. Without those spaces, I am more than capable of just blurting out any old thing, which can happen even with the spaces, but the chances decrease.

My admiration for poets is without limit. They are my magicians, well, along with musicians and those who write songs for they have their own language, a version of words unknown to the uninitiated. There is an aspect of writing that I think of as akin to moving furniture, if one had all the furniture in the world to choose from. Words arranged *just so* become image, metaphor. What the poets possess, the rest of us aspire to. It is not different than the alchemy of cooking, knowing what a pile of ingredients will taste like when combined. Words have their own alchemy, are their own alchemy, a wizard's tools, the wonder of letters stirred together to make *this*, Gregory Orr's "*lucid meaning*." We can always hope.

Skittish

Jumpy, nervous as in the skittish horse. In my case I think of it more as appropriately wary. Take nothing, or very little, for granted. It can be exhausting. The week past that had me resetting passwords all over the known virtual universe due to hacking or spamming of my address book causes me to approach my mailbox as though it might hold a nest of pit vipers.

Vigilance or hyper-vigilance are not desirable states. Excessive production of cortisol and other stress-related bodily responses is unwelcome not to mention unhealthy. I don't believe any living creature becomes skittish for no reason, as Mr. Edward Gorey points out—frequent ghastly happenings. Reversing skittish tendencies, there's the task.

The antidote for skittishness is, I suppose, peace, tranquility, or the ability to find and hold onto them in the midst of life being life. The waters cannot be trusted to grow still enough for a long enough time to count on that being the norm, the reliable, irrevocable norm. In the absence of which we must create our own calm or be forever tossed like kindling in a tornado. If we don't become our own placid centers we are at risk of rattling ourselves to bits, one bolt at a time. Soothing words spoken in gentle voices, reassuring touch, consistency, freedom from jeopardy or something else wearing its clothes, all help to sand smooth raw nerves and a tendency to yelp or tremble.

It is, we are or I am, like water in the locks of the Panama Canal, rising an increment at a time, making the transition from chronic jumpiness to a steady hand, no tea spilled in the saucer. How many movies have we seen where something spooks the horses, causes the herd to stampede? One of our broadcast channels shows Howard Hawkes' *Red River* about every 17 hours so I've been freshly reminded of the tendency to bolt at an unexpected sound, a sudden movement.

Human existence is rooted in the unexpected, which does not have to mean the alarming but merely that for which one has not planned. There have been and will probably continue to be long stretches when everything feels like a detour to me. Sink holes, landslides, *X Files*-like events, find another route. Unflappable is the goal—"*Be cool, my babies,*" as Conan O'Brien says—from stampede to serene in one lifetime.

To the doodlers, the daydreamers, the lost

Some words to ponder from Henry David Thoreau:

Not until we are lost
do we begin to understand ourselves.

In my land of curious synaptical leaps, this, of course, connects to doodling. I believe unshakably that our best focus comes down to the point of a pen or pencil. There are others who share and support this notion.

Between staring out the window, my splendid view being of treetops and the sky, and doodling, I am never more than inches from a pen and paper, I could easily be chosen Least Certain to Pay Attention in any group. I maintain it is more likely that our very best ideas and interpretations come from inner-generated concepts rather than from those forced upon us by the outside world

Doodling, or sky gazing, connect me to a fluid mental state where the obsessive and compulsive no longer exist. I am afloat on a vast Jules Verne-esque subterranean sea of imaginative no-thought. With no credentials whatsoever, I propose that we are the better, the saner, the more tranquil for time spent outside the company of conscious, purpose-filled thought. There are no lists in doodling, no clocks. The notion of *here* is in a state of flux, for we are free-wheelingly transported by a mind no longer under the influence of nine forward gears. (We seemed to get along very well with four, maybe five speeds, four plus overdrive in a 1956 Austin Healey 100-4. More has never meant the same as better.)

We may become lost through denial, avoidance, illness, forgetfulness, apathy, indifference and life being life. We get thrown off the bus, drummed out of the corps, abandoned, rejected, ignored, shunned and snubbed. We can also choose to be lost inside our daydreams or within the lines and shapes of doodles. Once removed from our thinking, ordinary-reality selves, we have time and space to encounter spirit. It is my theory that spirit always seeks to connect with us, to reach us beyond all that is busy and distracting, and will use whatever means are necessary. In my experience, spirit finds us through health-crises, through seismic shifts, through reversals of fortune if our attention can't be caught any other way. Or we can volunteer as doodlers and wool-gatherers and see what happens.

In her TED talk, Sunni Brown explains how doodling assists in retaining information, demonstrating how it is not a wasteful activity. Beyond that, I believe it aids us in uncovering information, allowing us access to collective knowledge or our own greater, undiscovered wisdom. By wandering away from ourselves, we are returned but at another level. Lost does not equate with emptiness. Lost is how we begin to fill.

Inhabit

> *Let us remember . . . that in the end we go to poetry for one reason, so that we might more fully inhabit our lives and the world in which we live them, and that if we more fully inhabit these things, we might be less apt to destroy both.*
>
> — Christian Wiman

The word, read this morning in Maria Popova's article in *The Marginalian* about Alan Watts and the antidote for anxiety, suggested to me aspects of comfort and ease, shoes off, shoulders relaxed, what my son calls "*chilling*," being at home, being home.

To inhabit our own lives, not sit like visitors on the edge of the sofa but sprawl, widens our understanding of ourselves, spread like water into every corner, dark or gleaming, is how presence begins. To inhabit is to spend time without squirming inside our own skin, in our own company, with our own thoughts. The word inhabit reminded me of being 17-18 years old, the degree to which I was lost and estranged and without hope only slightly diminished by recklessness and excess, yet I had a black cardigan in which I could simply be. It was long enough to reach the middle of my thighs, had deep pockets and an abundance that wrapped me up, sealed me. I was a walking blanket fort, undetectable, temporarily at peace, able to be in the world, an inhabitant.

Being present requires inhabiting the moment. I can't even bear the phrase multi-tasking, let alone the practice of it. Distracted and divided, how do we inhabit, for which we need the whole of us and not fragments, parts that can be spared from what seems more important. I know a number of friends with whom I talk on the phone are otherwise engaged while we converse. I don't take it personally, it is the way of things. But without being *here*, how do we claim the territory of our lives? Like homesteaders, we have to be on the land to call it ours. I will think further about the dimensions of inhabiting, the ways in which it demands a wholeness, an entirety, an awareness focused only on now.

The scope of the article is much broader than this week's word, though they share the same road. I love being in a world where wisdom lingers behind a headline, behind the columns in the parking garage, waiting to entice me with its eternal shiny newness, adjusting my perception.

Bygones

Any fans of the *Ally McBeal* series may remember Richard Fish (played by Greg Germann) dismissing any unpleasantness with the single word, bygones. As though that excused anything, everything. Life requires us to let go of so much.

Friends and lovers, family, homes, places, *things*. In weightier moments, the reality of how everything we treasure is really just on loan becomes unavoidable. That the bad times pass is the good news. That the good eventually follows them out of town is possibly why many of us trundle on in dual states of grief and contentment. Age only serves to make longer the list of what is gone.

One of my first friends lived next door in our post-War housing tract. Almost daily we played at my house but when my father arrived from work, his dinner awaiting, my mother would first tell Eva, kindly, it was time for her to go home. Each time Eva grabbed hold of the arm of the couch from which my mother then had to pry her four-year-old's fingers. Every time. I wonder now were there valid reasons why Eva would rather be with us, were we clueless about what might cause a child to fear her family. I will never know, but for 65 years Eva has been my model of how not to let go.

Through various chapters I've learned we cannot—or should not try to—make anyone stay who wishes to go. It suggests to me the same dark magic it would take to cause dead flowers to bloom again. Bygones. What is over is over.

It is not different with hurts, with slights or our own grievous, no matter how unintentional, errors. To keep them fresh, like a flagellant's wounds, has a sinister tinge. We ought not be the source of our own unhappiness. Holding on is just and only that.

More than 20 years ago I studied energy healing with a shaman. The training involved ritual, learning its power, becoming acquainted with symbolic actions. What I remember is writing—and rubber stamping images—on slips of tissue-thin paper, freezing them into an ice mold and allowing the ocean to melt the ice, release the woes, dissolve or carry them away. And what I remember is very soon after becoming as ill as I'd ever been, from which I am still recovering, and it taught me a lot about ritual not being for dabblers. Still. Being able to let go of what we stubbornly cling to or what seems to have epoxied itself to our spirit frees us for other business, better matters, new growth, evolution. I don't wish on anyone the job of prying my clinging fingers from that shadowy couch.

Sleep

Just as I was wishing for a spring tonic, thinking of old commercials for Geritol, I went to bed weary and befuddled, slept, and woke up renewed. It didn't last all day, not at the same strength as the zestful awakening, yet it was still miraculous.

Was there ever a more benevolent companion? It is the iron that smooths the wrinkles out of the most hopeless-seeming, too-new chambray shirt, the one that introduces, however briefly, the notion that cotton might be the enemy. Other parts of the day, regardless of the pleasure or sense of achievement they bring, are but phantom goodness compared to bedtime. There I sink into happy oblivion, knowing on the other side I will rise, a better version of myself, patient, clear-headed, no longer running on empty.

I am not a lovely sleeper. I know I drool, I know I snore, as a child I talked in my sleep and may still do so. My favorite clothes are as soft as ancient flannel pajamas. Until very recently—a habit to which I may return—I took a nap most afternoons. For the past week I haven't needed to get up quite as early and receive a nearly adequate amount of sleep without napping, though I believe there can never be too much.

I love sleep.
My life has the tendency
to fall apart when I'm awake, you know?

— Ernest Hemingway

The states induced by sleep help me hold onto a belief in parallel universes, astral travel. Unlike Hemingway, who may have been exaggerating, sleep is not the only part of my life with enough stick-um to keep things together, yet it seems to be the land in which the unlikely appears less so. Dreams, in full color and microscopic detail, feel like attending a festival of movies, in each of which I have a part. Because they frequently involve reunions with the departed, I may wake up with impossible longing for a little more time together.

Though dreams may leave me with a physical residue of emotions, I am mostly clueless as to their meaning, my best guess being only that. I push on hoping, trusting, that some of the wisdom they've deposited seeps through the veils into ordinary consciousness possibly manifesting as intuition, that unexplainable knowing which I am always willing to follow, even while questioning the advice.

Sleep heals and consoles, becomes Spackle for the fissures through which our waking dreams may seep and evaporate. Sleep finds the wallet we lost on the bus and returns it with contents intact, it shrinks time and distance and offers the keys to a city in which we are no older than our 40s, ever nimble, agile of mind, undimmed and have not yet given up on romance. No wonder I believe in magic.

Echoes

Duality marks our days, the simultaneous holding on and letting go, forever sifting, hoping to fit a disguise on our least-loved parts like a slipcover over an embarrassing chair. What I forget, what I assume many of us forget, is the way our golden child self echoes through the great din of real-life struggles. In hand-to-hand combat with minor vexations or challenges that loom larger than continents, we are not just hapless, aged grown-ups trying to be wise. Our child hearts, what we loved and love still, have not left us. In spite of the years, the decades of visible erosion brought on by illness and loss, trauma and circumstance, who we were at our most forgiving, optimistic, dream-fueled and gentle best remains to buoy us through dark waters.

When I am not fog-bound by the miasma of modern living, I am able to recognize, mostly through what resonates deeply, the presence of a surprisingly sturdy girl. She recently became clearer to me as I saw in my visiting brother the presence of a wonderful, wonder-filled boy not eclipsed in any way by the senior citizen costume he wears. As though he had smuggled the child in his suitcase, the boy stood by the dining table, reminding me with his bright smile of baseballs and fish caught, roads travelled, puzzles solved, early passions undimmed. Of course he became the man that he is, as did his friends, no longer adolescent wizards of automobile mechanics but grandfathers also for whom car talk will always be their first language.

It no longer feels so surprising that we prevail impossibly against tides and wind. These resilient young incarnations who have been with us, who *are* us, provide strength beyond our abilities of the moment. We are here because, no matter how it felt, we have not had to do this alone. Wearing a favorite turtle-print shirt or length of red cotton tied as a cape, they champion our causes, defend the banner. The child is father of the man, how did I not remember?

Gravitas

This morning I appeared to myself as a very old, at times nearly turgid river that passes through sights rarely seen, past bank-dwellers with snapping teeth and hides thick as textbooks. It is a somber business, life, confettied with tear-inducing laughter and cake-sweet moments of undiluted joy. We are meant to take it lightly and seriously not by turns as much as continuously, concurrently.

Gravitas, defined often as dignity, duty and seriousness, was considered perhaps the most foundational of the Roman virtues. For those of us who muddle, nearly blindfolded, through the 21st century, it speaks to living a purposeful life, showing dignity of character, possessing a deep-rooted seriousness. Gravitas, the grasp thereof, indicates that one knows the importance of the matter at hand.

In any given space and time, we are pinballed between the stupifyingly trivial and what is important, even weighty and grave. We are asked to abdicate witlessness and know the difference. The task has been set. To keep our hearts light while our minds grasp, and our demeanors reflect, the fact that we *get it* requires footwork the word fancy doesn't begin to describe.

This is not a goof, this span of years, not ours nor anyone's. Gravitas means not the absence of humor but the appropriate application of it.

Roses

For a time, until the aphids became more than anyone could bear, the porch of my childhood home was flanked by trellises through which pink climbing roses twined. We were not a gardening people. Everything was kept tidy by professionals who trimmed the hedges and mowed. I was elected for raking, sweeping and weeding. I once grew radishes and, as I remember, a few carrots for a class project. Never again a rose of any size or description.

In the last two years, perhaps less, rose images began courting me. And I such an easy mark. Beauty nourishes me and there is something about the rose, followed by flowers in general, that produces tranquility as I fall asleep, a lightness of heart when I'm awake. There is a sense akin to having made a new friend, one in whom affection and steadfastness are never doubted, whose ability to cheer does not falter.

I have reached and passed the age my sister once referred to as "powder-faced lady" from her long career in fashion and retail among the dowagers of Pasadena. As I picture them there is a hint of rose scent in their powder. I imagine a cut glass globe vase of the old varieties, petals loose and dreamy, not tightly furled like florist bouquets. A few petals have fallen, attractively, to the surface of a round, marble-topped table in the foyer, standing between twin staircases that curve to a second-floor balcony. Old world blossoms encouraged by loving hands.

So it is that I prowl Google's image library, entering the most accurate descriptions I can invent for what I hope to find, like rose-patterned socks.

It is encouraging, affirming, to fall so innocently in love with the enduring rose at an advanced age. No doubt I am not really so newly-smitten, that this hankering, this allegiance has lurked for some time, finally stepping into the light and declaring itself as the mad crush it is.

Events

At the high school across the street they have begun observing traditional June events, starting with the Sunday afternoon baccalaureate service. Graduation must be very near. Weddings, vacations, high points often originate in this prelude-to-summer month.

Difficult to say just when our events got under way. The first true milestone was that Sunday in early May when family, travelers from afar, arrived after a nearly 24-hour flight. We had not seen each other in 10 years. While they spent a week driving to and through parts of Northern California, we have had the unaccustomed joy of sitting together at the breakfast and dinner table. If there is no quote about laughter being the best seasoning, there ought to be. These are not ordinary days.

Some time ago our ancient apartment oven sparked itself into oblivion. We hoped to have its replacement in time for our guests, our event. The fact of its age and, accordingly, size made the search more lengthy than anticipated. Because time becomes one long and infinite loop of taffy for me, I think the new one was installed last Thursday, always welcome, never too late. It is a shiny creature and could probably challenge the computer on Jeopardy! I grow mute in its presence. Were it not built into the cabinet, we might have done a welcome dance around it.

It has been a time of domestic evolution, the coming-going of household objects in addition to the ovens from a Swiffer mop, handsome piece of furniture and entertainment electronics to broke-ass office chairs, a manual treadmill and sectional of advanced decrepitude and missing springs that we'd had no hope of ever seeing jettisoned. The amount of drama involved with having new things come in up a precarious flight of stairs—the floating kind with nothing solid keeping them all in the air—and, more to the point, going down them to await curbside pickup exceeded any expectation I had.

Phone calls, financial negotiations, further phoning, a self-appointed mayor of our block who was displeased with our unsightly sofa parts and demanded the movers relocate them, more phoning, more arranging. And then, last Tuesday, the sound of the behemoth rubbish truck pulling away after I heard our discards clanking into its formerly empty recesses one at a time. It's enough to make you want to kiss everybody.

The events roll on and include this week two NBA finals games which we hope to watch together, unless our visitors have an invitation too tasty to miss. I am doing my best not to think of their departure, the one event I would put off like the master procrastinator I am. Until then, picture us at the table with its blooming orchids centerpiece surrounded by coupons for take-out food. I think this is pizza night.

Ensorcelled

At the top of my soul food pyramid sits beauty, sometimes known by the name color. I am no longer sure what is the pointy part, what is the flat part, are grains good or out of favor? What I know is that I am nourished by, sustained by and captivated by beauty as I define it.

As with others who know enchantment, I am pulled away from useful tasks, necessary maintenance of ordinary life, by images that speak to me. I blame the internet, I blame my own curiosity about tracking things down, I especially blame Pinterest. Yet in the same breath I thank all those for access to wonders I could not possibly have known, if these seemingly magic connections did not exist.

They tell us at World Wide Word that we are not likely to find "ensorcelled" in our daily newspaper, that it is a word more often chosen for poetry, literature or sword-and-sorcery fantasies. It is descriptive, ensorcelled, not a passive act but one of intention and power. Beauty in all its forms refuses to leave us napping. It has come to feed our hungry hearts, nurse wan souls back to health, lift us from lethargy and gloom, banish indifference. Take as many helpings a day as you can manage. Beauty, you sorceress, abundant, underrated resource, calls and suggests we may as well hide our watches, stop our clocks. Beneath her radiance, time becomes meaningless.

Part II

Unseen

In his short story, "The Night the Bed Fell on Father," James Thurber wrote of a character who piled her belongings outside the bedroom door at night with instructions that any burglars take what they wanted and not use their chloroform on her. We are fragile vessels on endless, unknowable seas taking what precautions we can and hoping for the best. Such a grain, a particle of what exists falls within our scope, so much is unseen.

On a solo Alaskan hunting trip in what I imagine to be a vast snowy wasteland, my Uncle Ray was, after a number of days, picked up as had been arranged. When the pilot landed, he told Ray that he could see from the air what Ray could not have known: that he was being stalked by a polar bear. This may be family myth, I may have misremembered all or part of it.

I experience life as an act of faith, an unspooling continuum in which what we must know next somehow finds us, steps forward, states its name. So much of the unseen is the good, which may leave itself like notes written in a spidery and nearly illegible hand tucked under a corner of the doormat. A whiff of night-blooming jasmine, possibly imagined for the plant is no longer there, drifting through the second floor window. Our sight is enhanced by distance of time and space. I've heard often in 12-step meetings, "More will be revealed." And it will, it is. Meanwhile, unless we wish to suffer needlessly, we operate as advised by Rainer Maria Rilke:

> *Be patient toward all that is unsolved in your heart and try to love the questions themselves, like locked rooms and like books that are now written in a very foreign tongue. Do not now seek the answers, which cannot be given you because you would not be able to live them. And the point is, to live*

everything. Live the questions now. Perhaps you will then gradually, without noticing it, live along some distant day into the answer.

Note to self: befriend the unseen. Think of ways in which to do this.

Circles

Duality continues to muscle us this way and that. As we cross thresholds of age, the circles expand and the circles narrow. The spirals coil tighter.

In widening, influences create ripples that reach further from the center, they encompass and include more. We exceed our imagined limitations, find our shells not the rigid corrals that kept us in and the world out. Not shells at all but sheer encasings akin to jelly fish, billowing and pliant like crepe paper though entirely waterproof, stretched into cupped shapes. They are meant to contain. We open to and accommodate the simple, the rare, the true in manifestations we could not even name as recently as yesterday. The universe becomes a child seated in the shopping cart, pulling exotic treats off the shelves while we try to stick to our meticulous and budget-minded lists.

As we reach *detente* with what remains unanswerable or unresolvable within, we require a smaller spool upon which to wind our ribbons. Earlier lack of clarity that insisted upon swirling acreage to navigate within finds altered interpretations. Furor hogs the bed, fills the room, spills into the yard and floods the fields. Harmony, without fidgeting, sits on a footstool and keeps its hands to itself.

The soul as a bellows, air drawn in, air expelled. Within our circles we are enlarged and reduced. I am reminded:

> *Be infinitely flexible and constantly amazed.*
>
> — Jason Kravitz

> *The measure of intelligence is the ability to change.*
>
> — Albert Einstein

Summer

The wide, free days of childhood summers glow with their own light. The sun rides higher in the sky, convincing us that sleeping in is a wasteful act, for who would choose to miss the hours of deep morning shadows, the long-absent joy of shorts?

Reading and summer remain forever paired, beginning with a weekly stack of picture books from the library, evolving to whatever we wished to sample from the family bookshelves. It was the season in which I discovered Carson McCullers and for years re-read southern writers then, aligning myself with the heat from their fiction. The temperature also matched tales from Ray Bradbury's *The Illustrated Man.*

> *Prologue*
>
> *It was a warm afternoon in early September when I first met the Illustrated Man. Walking along an asphalt road, I was on the final leg of a two weeks' walking tour of Wisconsin. Late in the afternoon I stopped, ate some pork, beans, and a doughnut, and was preparing to stretch out and read when the Illustrated Man walked over the hill and stood for a moment against the sky.*
>
> *. . . Though it was a hot late afternoon, he wore his wool shirt buttoned tight about his neck. His sleeves were rolled and buttoned down over his thick wrists. Perspiration was streaming from his face, yet he made no move to open his shirt.*
>
> *. . . The pictures were moving, each in its turn, each for a brief minute or two. There in the moonlight, with the tiny tinkling thoughts and the distant sea voices, it seemed, each*

little drama was enacted. Whether it took an hour or three hours for the dramas to finish, it would be hard to say. I only know that I lay fascinated and did not move while the stars wheeled in the sky.

I doubt if statistics support my belief that there exists a time of year in which imagination grows richer, sprouts, then broadcasts its seeds which take root and repeat the process. Space and time, two Bradbury themes, describe summer as I knew it in childhood, as I know it now in retirement. I give thanks for the luxury of a wandering mind, never lost but now able to poke along unexplored paths I had to pass up when real life held me more rigidly in its grip.

Extravagance

To the better angels of my nature I give credit for tenacity, for the gradual softening of inclinations toward stinginess, fear of lack. Mostly that, fear of there not being enough. Their wise counsel, laid upon my heart, urges me more toward extravagance, not as a vice but a virtue. While extravagance appears as a synonym for profusion, words more suggestive of unhealthy excess are given as matches for extravagance.

We are meant, I am certain, to be extravagant, lavish, with our kindness. Not the giving everyone in the audience a new car version of lavish, but the sort that we call upon to lift one another up, placing that before any imagined safety, any automatic smallness of our spirit. We are here to be the gown with too many ruffles, the dessert buffet that never ends, the speakers and spreaders of love that one can sink into. Deep love.

Deciding that we will not offer meager rations of anything within our power to give frees us from the gnawing suspicion that we may be jerks. I swear those angels sidle up with quiet golf claps when I realize and admit to unworthy behavior, even if I'm the only one who knows the extent of its pettiness. *Largesse* feels wonderful, no matter what the commodity. For a moment, we do without so another can have more. It can make such a difference. We find ourselves restored, replenished by practicing immoderation, by learning to be preposterous with our love, our compassion, our attending to needs of others rather than our own in ways small or large.

Fear, its power to drag us out of the moment and into a bleak and uncertain future, is profusion's vampire. It would see us shriveled, shrunken, tightly coiled and isolated. We are urged, "Don't be delicate, be vast and brilliant." Embrace extravagance, it suits you.

Musings

If you think color is not an enchantress, will not lure you away from wherever you are needed and seduce you into a reverie, a fugue state, then your infatuation is much more under control than mine. For those of us whose color-centered musings are lengthy and frequent, we have what might be called a spokesman. In his book, *The Primary Colours: Three Essays*, Alexander Theroux spins along every path that red, yellow or blue ever trod or dreamed of treading until we are nearly dizzy. In the very best sense.

Of the book, *Publishers Weekly* said, "Theroux's dazzling, free-form meditation explores the three primary colors through their myriad associations in art, history, music, poetry, fiction, movies, anthropology, linguistics, myth, religion, science, food, sports, and everyday life."

From the dust jacket we read, "There is poetry here; there is also song, fable, opinion, literary criticism, gossip, history, and fascinating fact—a fund of *curiosa*, gleanings of a witty and penetrating mind."

To give you an example from Yellow with regard to complexions, Theroux writes, "It all put me in mind of creepy Mrs. Danvers in du Maurier's *Rebecca* and that one hideously arresting detail I've never forgotten: 'I could see how tightly the skin was stretched across her face, showing the cheek-bones. There were little patches of yellow'—shudder—'beneath her ears.' " He tells us that detective Sam Spade and Rosemary's baby had yellow eyes.

As the possessor of facts on all matters, Theroux may be without equal. How much of the information he shares as musings on these three colors came from his own memory, how much from research for the project we have no way of knowing. And it doesn't matter in the least. The way he hopscotches from one exploration to another keeps me sprinting after him, marveling at how limited my thoughts on such a favored subject have been. In case I ever exhaust, which seems unlikely, all he can tell me about the primary colors, another volume, *The Secondary Colors: Three Essays*, awaits.

Meanwhile, consider this:

> *No animal has blue fur.*
>
> — Alexander Theroux

Chimerical

As my art for the past 20 years has been primarily involved with designing rubber stamps, there have been, of necessity, lines around everything I do. Recently my thoughts, and heart, have shifted to a more chimerical presentation. I have a deep hunger for what is more flowing, more created of smoke, of vapor, of what may be at least partly imagined, of dreams. As I fall asleep, I imagine paintings as yet non-existent, yet distinct enough to be seen by the mind's eye.

The art of Francoise de Felice, which I found just a few weeks ago, is the manifestation of what seemed too ethereal to become solid matter. That her images are women, the women we may be in our own memories or dreams, the embodiment of the numinous with which we seek enduring connection, draws me even more fully into this world, a world I know though I cannot say from where, or when.

In the process of maturing or evolving or being prodded into consciousness, I feel we are asked to fall in love with ourselves as we never have. The scenes, the groupings which de Felice brings to full, robust, soft and not-quite-solid life give me the sense of seeing a self that is at once idealized and yet authentic. Her women are dimensional in a way that seems to have little to do with day-to-day experiences of hacked passwords, overdue medical procedures, ants in the kitchen, as though they have found the secret to existing outside the limitations of time, space and what is expected of the rest of us.

They inspire me about my work, they make me feel illuminated from within rather than standing in some external spotlight whose glare is just too harsh. If I am one of them, I am not just shadows, lines, creases and age. I am timeless, I am beauty, I am depth and

I am not too late for anything that matters. Though they, in their softness, may seem chimerical, they are the reality in which I choose to believe, the world I prefer to inhabit. Perhaps some illusions are actually life affirming. I believe these are.

Communion

If having a soul means being able to feel love and loyalty and gratitude, then animals are better off than a lot of humans.

— James Herriot, *All Creatures Great and Small*

This week my Facebook feed was alive with animal videos and I watched them all. As I am allergic to cats and dogs, I don't have extensive first-hand experience of communion with other creatures. Being, at least, a reasonably observant human I understand the depth of such love, of such relationships. In the recent past, too many friends have lost beloved companions. Grief is grief. It is not exclusive to a particular species.

I wondered, briefly, about my sudden affinity for watching cats, dogs, penguins and unidentified small birds being remarkable. I realized their presence gave comfort. That their presence was virtual made a connection to them no less real. A dog splashing water on beached fish, attempting to revive them, astonished me. A cat luxuriating in a lengthy massage, paws, chin, ears, head, torso, made me grateful there was such an attuned and caring friend.

Being human and being a grown-up carry similar responsibilities. The guy driving the car has made a covenant with fellow creatures to be sober, attentive, safe, as wise as possible, compassionate, trustworthy, and to alert someone if these conditions can't be met. We know it doesn't always play out as this ideal. Watching and absorbing the significance of interaction with our furred and winged fellows, observing their unambiguous responses, the result of their communion, elevated my consciousness, informed me, softened and humbled me. I am still digesting what I saw, what the videos were teaching me, why this seems to be a lesson needed NOW. Today the answers are still arriving at their pace, not mine.

There is no such thing as too much love, the real deal and not some *poseur*. Love without guile, expectations, conditions and limits, how and where do we find that. Surprisingly—or not—Facebook for all its drawbacks may have offered a clue.

Reimagine

Today I declare that imagination is our top and truly kick-ass superpower. As with other endowments, it may be used for good or ill. Today I declare it is no longer appropriate to employ imagination to enlarge or inflate fear or worry, to use it as the magnifying glass that sharpens a focus on our suspected defects, to bend it to our will for the purpose of keeping us frail or tepid or less-than. We, as Werner Herzog reminded in a recent interview, are able to give success our own definition and we certainly are here to save the world by whatever means possible. This will involve stealth, humor, beauty, love and patience.

Without being vast and brilliant, saving the world, even a section no larger than a collar button, would be impossible. Therefore, we must reimagine, redefine what we believe about ourselves and how we fit into this world that needs us at our truest. Recently I found a quote by writer Paulo Coelho, "Don't be intimidated by other people's opinions. Only mediocrity is sure of itself, so take risks and do what you really want to do." As the loudest voice of disapproval is usually the one in our own heads, that is the first one to ignore. Sing louder than it shouts. Make faces and do a silly dance. Righteous mediocrity can't stand any of that. And, above all else, throw your arms around every lumpy, battle-scarred, making-it-up-as-you-go-along inch of your brilliant being and squeeze until you can hardly breathe. Don't let go. I'm not saying this will be easy. It may seem impossible, but, as Coelho also said, "Impossible is just an opinion.""

In our reimagining, let's imagine this: that most of what we've been told is wrong or, even more likely, was lies intended to keep us quiet, submissive, to stop us from being troublemakers and siphon our unmistakable coolness out of the tank, leaving us stuck and dispirited.

I realized this week, in visiting some top-drawer work from artist Lisa Congdon and writer Maria Popova on women who have changed the way we see the world, that it is, at this late date, unlikely that I will be (a) famous or (b) brilliant on the BIG screen. That does not mean I am not or cannot be brilliant. The stars come in all sizes. Brilliant, and successful, by my definition. Some days all that requires is being alive, reasonably awake and aware that none of us is ordinary, unless we choose to be. Imagine something brighter, something better, something that makes your heart happy, not lurching along with grim foreboding. No one has ever known what will come tomorrow. I imagine it, and we, will be magnificent.

Passion and curiosity

For three nights this week we watched documentaries, having completed all episodes of *The Sopranos* and the brief third season of *The Killing*. As one day spooled into the next, I thought I spotted similarities among the films, themes that were shrieking, mutedly, in my own life. My son's life as well. On Saturday night our choice was a 2014 release called *Particle Fever*, following the completion and launch of the Hadron Collider with the hope of explaining the origin of matter. In the film scientists frequently discuss how long they have been searching for, waiting for this answer. It illuminates impatience over drying ink or paint as the microscopically trivial matter it is.

On the previous nights, we watched *The Battered Bastards of Baseball* which follows the impossible arc of one man's dream, to own a winning minor league ball team, and *Valentino, The Last Emperor* during which we get to attend the extravagant gala that marked the designer's retirement after 45 years as a man who made women look beautiful.

Where the three stories intersect is that each, as I interpret it, was fueled and sustained by passion along with a curiosity, a refusal to leave until it is known how each drama turns out. This is where my writer son and I could see ourselves, aware that if we don't write whatever has demanded us as its authors, neither we nor anyone will learn what happens.

We are called by some unlikely sirens, passion sparked by thoughts of a white pastel pencil in one moment, a scalloped circle paper punch in the next, while a dimly-lit slide show of text and images plays in the background. However odd we may find these sequential obsessions, we would be fools to ignore their allure. They call for a reason. They may be considered pieces of passion, separate elements that will join forces when all have been collected, not unlike the thousands of scientists involved with the collider project, each an essential part, each bringing what they have to obtain the elusive answer.

The line between passion and obsession may become blurry, we may ask ourselves is this folly or wisdom and we may not be able to respond. What we do know is this: if we dismiss curiosity and intuition, decide not to follow the trail however poorly marked, we will never learn what it, what we, might have been.

Filter

We are each, for how could we not be, filters of experience and information. What happens to us is sifted, strained, clarified, and transmuted. Whether or not this is more true for anyone who creates I don't know. All is process.

Taking exception to something I find on the internet is one of my least favorite, as it is so unproductive, things even to contemplate. When I found Buzzfeed's "25 quotes that will inspire you to be a fearless writer" I knew I'd been challenged to a duel. Generally (my interpretation) the quotes suggest that unless the story we tell is autobiographical, we are cowards. I disagree.

I have told my story to friends, in 12-step meetings, in recovery groups, in therapy and I no longer find any benefit, for me or anyone, in telling it. However, being a highly porous collection of particles and/or energy, by filtering it over time it has become something else, I hope something possibly more useful and more entertaining. I assume, being optimistic that way, it will be more than one story. Its current shape is the episodic fiction that found me, I was not seeking it, that follows the summer activities of residents in the coastal town, Billington's Cove, particularly Gloria who owns the tea room and Robert Apotienne, aka The Reading Man, who is vacationing in the Cove.

How everything I've ever experienced, heard, read, seen or imagined was refined into now nearly 70 episodes of this quiet tale is one of my personal Great Mysteries. Yet this is the truth of it. Plants take in sunlight and convert it to chlorophyll. Or something like that. If we are very lucky, we turn lead into gold.

If you create, fashion by whatever means something that has not existed before, I find it impossible to believe there is one right way to do it. There are writers who bleed on the page, whose clear calling is to tell us exactly how it was, how it is. There are others who send us tumbling down rabbit holes or leave us in strange company on desert planets. Paint what calls to you, what demands your hand and no other. Write the world that has taken up residence within. I will survive being thought a coward, should I ever arrive at a place where critics get their hands on my work. I am done being scolded.

Becalmed

My sister has a name for it, that first morning when you *know* summer has folded its tent and crept out of town, leaving the beaches, the hills and the cities to the spell of fall. She calls it The Snap. We in Southern California are nowhere near The Snap or even its second cousin. It may have come to those of you in other climes. Even if the weather warms again for any duration, The Snap, once declared, is absolute. My son and I have traded Jack Nicholson's memorable line from *Terms of Endearment*, "I was inches from a clean getaway," to rue the arrival of hot days, one upon another, after what we hoped would continue to be a mild summer, all summer. Alas.

I speak of it mostly because how un-Snap our days became seems to have becalmed a portion of me, turned me increasingly leaden and dull-witted as the week advanced. Life is cycles and if the weather plays a part, I can't say. I have almost reached the border where staring and drooling become virtues. In a world of strife, disasters, losses and alarms this is nothing, a mere bagatelle, and its unimportance is almost too embarrassing to mention. Yet knowing where we are, creatively, emotionally, physically and otherwise, seems like good sense. We will not be the same every day. I would not be surprised to learn that last week's massive solar flare has put me off my, let's call it, game. Between that unknown influence and a full super moon, who knows what havoc they shower on such beings as we.

The possibility that I was intended to be a hibernating creature does not seem impossible. It may be that, even without The Snap, my nature has already begun to slow me down in preparation for being packed into a box of dry leaves and stored in the laundry room for the duration, as my family did with our desert tortoises each year. This will pass, as will our scorching days.

Before long, one morning when the slanting sun casts palm tree-shaped shadows on our stucco home, we will know it is here at last. Welcome home to The Snap. We are never entirely peaceful until you arrive.

Foretell

As a younger creature, I wished to know what life held for me. Consulting, even infrequently, psychics, readers of runes and such had two fatal drawbacks: it cost too much money and the ones I consulted must have found me unreadable. The conclusion I reached is that I was not meant to know. Such information would be far more curse than blessing, I can see that now. But once it felt intensely important to know if there would be a happy ending. In the absence of knowing what would come next, the other option was to prepare for any eventuality, which we know is not possible. For many years I described myself as "a belt AND suspenders" type. There are no guarantees.

Recently I was referred to a website as the source for uncommon words related to color. The site, The Phrontistery, meaning a thinking place, has gathered obscure, forgotten and little-used language for an array of subjects of which color is just one. Another was "Divination and Fortune-telling." Oh ho. So many untried avenues, unexplored methods by which to foretell. So many caught my attention but I think the best match would be stichomancy, "divination by picking passages from books at random." Reaching for the book closest to the keyboard, a swell volume called "Beach Beauties: Postcards and Photographs 1890–1940," I found this on the first page I turned to:

> *Of course, postcards are notoriously unreliable.* (is this a clue?) *While they can serve as the cultural historian's dream, they are also sometimes creative works of fiction.*

How to interpret this? As the Magic 8-Ball might say, "Signs unclear, ask again later." I don't believe there was a single category for "divination by intuition."

What awaits is information beyond our knowing and for good reasons. Hope and possibilities keep us showing up. Predictions and proclamations are highly mutable. I like to think that most doors remain open, in spite of what experts tell us, even those practiced in tyromancy, "divination using cheese." I rest my case.

Pond

It is larger than a puddle, not as large as a lake and is thought, by consensus, to be a small body of still water. On a good day, it could be my mind.

"A capacity for stillness" was not an attribute I could have named until I came to know my son and saw in him what I might never have seen in myself. For all my twitches and human shortcomings, I have for my whole life been able to become quiet and spend time in my own company without screaming.

A pond, a pondering pool, unruffled water beside which one might sit in dreamy idleness. Spirits and faeries would gather on its banks. Their just-missed presence could be detected by the prints of their leaf-shaped slippers where the ground was moist. Fall asleep there and faerie mischief might weave vines and trumpet-shaped flowers in your hair. They might take your best silver ring, either to guarantee your return to look for it or as fair barter for the bits of magic they tuck into your pocket, pin to your lapel.

We move beyond time when near a pond. The deeper the shade, the thicker the moss, the farther we have wandered from what is ordinary, burdensome and dulling about everyday life. Unlike the hypnotic, stirring motion of the sea, a pond abides. The ocean waits, it can wait forever, yet it paces and prowls, roams and returns. A pond is undemanding, certain we will arrive exactly where we are meant to be without its prodding. A calm presence, it trusts our wisdom. What it reflects turns us back to ourselves, our secret chambers of longing, our wishes, our dreams.

I leave you with these two quotes by Henry David Thoreau:

I learned this, at least, by my experiment; that if one advances confidently in the direction of his dreams, and endeavors to live the life which he has imagined, he will meet with a success unexpected in common hours.

and

However mean your life is, meet it and live it; do not shun it and call it hard names.

Floribunda

Characterized by large flowers, growing in clusters, floribunda roses are hybrids. It seems the word may also refer to other plants with copious and showy blossoms. The sublime in bunches, nothing stingy, pure generosity.

If we have lessons to learn from the moth, the earthworm, the oak, the tide, I have no doubt that roses are our teachers as well. Be beautiful in your own unique way, be an explosion of what feels extravagant and lovely. It does not require external assistance. It is about your essential self flowering in and out of season. Carlos Castaneda said:

> *The spirit listens only when the speaker speaks in gestures. And gestures do not mean signs or body movements, but acts of true abandon, acts of largesse, of humor. As a gesture to the spirit, warriors bring out the best of themselves and silently offer it to the abstract.*

If coming into bloom isn't an act of true abandon, then I am not sure what is.

I will speak for myself, knowing that I am not alone in this: I believe we too easily under-value our worth and worth may manifest in such subtle forms. The mere sight of a rose delights and, surprisingly perhaps, reassures me. All has not turned to dust, to despair. I find such hope in the bright and fragrant (real or imagined) splendor of a rose or its bud. It is a botanical marvel. Be as the rose, the poets might say, bringing to any situation such gifts as humor, compassion, attentiveness, insight, kindness, generosity, wit, sparkle, gravitas, foolishness, honesty, presence, for that which the heart or eye or spirit finds pleasing is you in full flower.

Think of your most glorious, abundant self as a modest daisy if you wish, a wee violet, but remember there are no small gifts. In our quiet ways we are heady, billowing, profuse and possess the ability to turn soured milk sweet. We are that amazing and powerful, capable of serious magic.

Roundup

Eventually, if we are lucky, age arrives to welcome us to its club. In the process of reaching this status, we may notice that parts of ourselves take on aspects of socks lost to laundromats in cities almost too numerous to mention. This past week I received gifts that aided in the roundup of some cherished bits from a specific time and I had not been conscious they were even missing. A formal definition of "roundup" suggests a systematic gathering of scattered people and things. Mine was roundup of happenstance.

As brief a backstory as I can assemble: A few weeks ago, in correspondence with a friend of some years, she told of locating, she thought, the issue of a long discontinued craft magazine (*American Home Crafts*) for which she had designed a needlework project. After reading her mail, I did a search of my own to see if I could find any additional magazines. What I found was a blogger who had, as of the writing, unearthed a few random copies in a thrift store. She shared photos of some pages and there was my friend's work. The flurry of additional emails brought the two of them together. I posted on Facebook about the much missed publication and a project I had done from one of their patterns. I told that my collection of every issue from debut to *au revoir* had not made a crucial move some 22 years ago and of my regret for that oversight.

The Facebook post sparked its own dialogue with a most generous friend who believed she still had all the copies she collected, as I had, in the 1970s. In short, after I described the pages I longed for, she found and copied and sent them to me. What I remembered as a blue chambray Levi's work shirt brightened with embroidered flowered vines was, in fact, an off-white shirt in the magazine photo, which she had sent ahead to confirm we were both in the right neighborhood.

In case this sounds like much ado over nothing, I need to say that *American Home Crafts* was unlike any craft magazine seen before or, really, since. The photography, the imagination of projects, the pure style made one want to tackle things they'd never done before. It truly was a case of "the best of us," and I dove into the satin stitch pattern worked in variegated DMC threads with enthusiasm. That was nearly 40 years ago.

When the pages arrived in their manilla envelope, I had no idea what sort of fish I'd gotten hold of. Seeing the pages connected me to the much younger woman I was then, the life I was living, the then-husband for whom the shirt was created and produced a telescoping of time that allowed my now rather senior self to delight again in the inspiration of the magazines, eagerly awaited every six months, and the sense of accomplishment at trying something beyond what I thought was my skill level. It was a cellular experience, feeling both of us within the same skin, as though I had taken one simple step backward and gathered up at least some of those missing socks.

Part III

Words

One of the questions asked of botanical alchemist India Flint, in a published interview was: What is your favorite word?

Is it possible to name just one and, if so, how long would it take you to narrow it down? Pretty much forever would be my answer.

I like the word *escarpment* which I believe I first heard in the original *King Kong*.

Some words resonate for the sound they make, the way they shape the mouth, the exercise of pronouncing them. Others are favored for their meaning, such as *ponder*, which I use almost constantly, or *languid* which I employ less often but am always looking for the right occasion.

The names of colors—*crimson, heliotrope, chartreuse, ebony, marigold*—feel like playmates whom one could invite to a tea party. Do you ever think about changing your name? I did, just now.

Squelchy or sharp-edged words appeal, such as *quagmire* and *barnacle*. Because they are visual, I am fond of *billow* and *trudge*.

For the naming of fictional characters, I believe Charles Dickens is a master. I give you *Uriah Heep, Mrs. Malaprop, the Murdstones.* Sometimes you can tell a book by its cover.

Flexible

Our experiences turn us into teachers. They also turn us flexible, cause us to finds ways to prevail in the real world and not the one of our fantasies. We are water, we are streams whose natural paths are clogged, blocked by debris or the work of zealous beavers. We find our way. We may be slowed, we are not stopped.

It is within the past eight years, perhaps less, that I have come to know myself as an adaptive creature. The ways I once moved, walked, cooked, the ways I once lived have vanished. Those ways have been replaced by the next best thing. I marvel at and give thanks for substitutions, support devices which began with a cane, my own unexpected capacity for adjusting and the previously unnoticed corners into which this turn of events has shined a light. I have come to believe that we all live, in some fashion, adaptively. That there is any life where all is perfection seems unlikely.

Another belief of mine is that we are here to give comfort and encouragement to each other, to bring the good we possess and share it as widely as possible. Our disappointments and the ways in which we cope with, even triumph over them help us write our playbook of clever, though perhaps awkward-looking tricks. That we must all cope with something we didn't choose unites us. Fighting what is unwanted will not make it go away but it will embitter us and wear us out. Better to maximize the skills, the strengths we still possess.

Yet another belief (maybe I should just have made a list) is that we are not meant to be defeated by the charging rhinoceros, singular or plural, that upended our plans. That onslaught becomes part of the equation, part of us, of our experience. We ignore or exclude it at our peril. How much better to make it, if not an ally, then at least a consultant. Illness, injury, affliction have demands, the first one being a course correction. If we are able to continue, more or less, in the direction we were going when we met the rhinoceros on the road, we will at the very least be going at a different pace, probably taking a detour, maybe hunkering in place while the dust settles.

The human spirit, with which we are field-equipped, survives disappointment. It survives jolts and losses, the forces of nature and time and our own unrealized dreams. We redraw the boundaries, surrender expectations in favor of a general trust in the good outcome, find comfort in what is and try not to keep breaking our own hearts over and over by dwelling on what is not.

Variables

We live in a two-story, pink stucco building which has the word "Capri" as part of its name on the facade. The color and name make giving directions easier, make it harder to miss Other apartments on the block are less emphatic. And I'll bet they don't have pink bathtubs.

Yet our Capri quarters lose any exotic cachet, however slight, when compared to the varying shades of blue in Morocco's once-secret mountain city of Chefchaouen. As I am so eternally drawn to colors, I wonder what variables may be at work as influences on mind and spirit in a blue city. Think of it.

It could be a direct line of descent from the Puritan Ethic that has kept my inner bohemian in mostly subdued wrappers for so long, always leaning toward, longing for deeply saturated hues as displayed in other lands, in clothing, in doorways.

One could not possibly remain unchanged, going from shades of black to combinations of lime peel, mango and blueberry. One can imagine the magnitude of shift made possible by changing the vista from politely, quietly American ordinary to the distantly, almost other-worldly vivid. I know I feel happier, I feel more myself when I wear anything that is a true red. Coloring my grey hair became too frequent and wearying a task though I know I would be altered by seeing a once-again red-haired version of myself looking back from the mirror.

I've written before that color is a language to me. It is also a vitamin, a tonic, an essential nutrient, a form of rescue and helium in the dirigible by means of which I will make my getaway. I may dream of Morocco's blue city, a round table next to the open windows, sipping a glass of golden tea while afternoon haze merges with shadowed robin's egg stairways before the market closes.

Playing for time

There is a sensibility with which I identify in the work of artists Kirsty Elson and Michelle Holmes. Their wooden seaside encampments and understated embroidered vignettes express visually some of what I hope to capture in the ongoing story on my blog of *Gloria and The Reading Man.* In the saga of 60-some episodes (so far), I arrived at a pivotal moment and its details have not yet become clear.

Because the characters and their place found me, not the other way around, I've learned to be trusting and patient. They will spill the beans when they are ready. They resist, which I've come to respect, any of my attempts to give them false moments, contrived musings, inauthentic action. They and their setting do not belong to ordinary reality as to time and space. I consider them not only imaginary friends but more. They seem able to gauge the tides of my heart and inform me accordingly. I have come to know myself better through them. With their help I am clearer about what I believe, how the world, the universe even, works.

What happens after the dance, I mean THE DANCE, I have no idea. It is not the ultimate moment in their story, yet it is much more than just a moment. My great wish is that I not muddy any part of it by rushing them.

Once upon a time I meditated daily. In the way of things, I somehow grew apart from that beneficial practice. In the last few weeks, joining Oprah and Deepak Chopra, I've found what may be the way back to the states of mind that result from meditation. My first thought was unattractively judgmental. After the first session, I was grateful for the ease of the exercise. It may be the lazy woman's path and I'm fine with that. My rather elderly joints and muscles need comfort in order to focus. I am either dreaming more or am more aware of my dreams. I've had moments of being more connected to aspects of myself that I forgot existed. I am able to slip into a state of detachment from daily stuff and let images appear, either during the meditation or other parts of the day.

In one of these "states," I saw a younger Reading Man standing in a field, talking in a soft animal voice to a horse for whom he obviously had great affection. Their heads together, they seemed halves of the same whole. Any stilling of the chattering, fretting mind allows the veil to thin. I love going there.

I hope it won't be too much longer before my undeclared lovebirds and I resume our adventure. I think of them as absent friends or a phantom limb, not as inventions of my imagination. Until we meet again.

Wonderstruck

That at any hour on any day I may find (figuratively) my knees weakened by the sight or knowledge of a previously unknown delight for the eye or mind or spirit or, generally, all of the above, causes me to declare myself permanently wonderstruck.

Learning of the Hari Kuyo festival yesterday via the writing of Mister Finch, himself a wonder, then discovering the date of the annual festival is February 8, my birthday, set all my senses tingling. I was brought to speechlessness by a celebration so profound and humble. Thinking of all we owe to—would we call them service objects?—and to our own hands as the means of livelihood, the means of keeping ourselves and our families fed and clothed, transported, protected, educated and entertained, my heart sighed for women.

It is celebrated by a woman in Japan as a memorial to all the sewing needles broken in their service in the past year. They gather at shrines and temples with needles and pins, which are stuck into tofu or soft jelly cakes. Prayers are said for improved skills.

I hear the sound of monks chanting as women approach the block of tofu, the place of rest for tired tools, and long for such ceremony, such acknowledgement of the sacred in daily life. My message is that we need to create our own rituals, build the habit of reverence for what may be deemed small and insignificant yet is anything but. Artists, think of pens, brushes, scissors, think of lined yellow tablets or typewriters or keyboards, think of ink but continue to think of needles, of pins. The work of creating, of connecting, of holding together, preserving, mending, think of its significance, its metaphor.

Reading of this festival caused me to look at my hands, offer thanks for how well they learned the skills necessary to care for myself, my family, to create, to embellish, to add color and silliness and surprise in unexpected corners. When we become wonderstruck, we are shifted on our foundations, pushed to the often teetering edge of the unknown where the only known element is awareness of wonder, that we are not who we were a moment ago.

Seasonal ambivalence

Even before Thanksgiving the fidgeting part of my brain started making trouble. It decided the only thing that would *feel* like the Christmas it thought it needed was to have it be 1958 again. I could be 13, my 8-year-old sister and I could ride the bus downtown to shop at the dime stores, then have cokes and grilled cheese sandwiches for lunch at Woolworth's counter. Even though I'd be past the age of actually, actually believing in Santa, I would still be years away from being able to sleep through the night on Christmas eve.

It is the same fidgeting subdivision that started a feud with Christmas after my son was terribly ill in the hospital for most of December eight years ago. The lights, the music on the radio, the sight of shoppers or diners through restaurant windows as I drove home to our empty apartment all those nights became intolerable. I didn't want to be reminded of a fear so deep. Christmas became the fall guy. Which, as I was cluelessly unaware, made his first, second, etc., Christmas less than festive for my son who only wanted to celebrate as normally, joyfully, as possible after his ordeal. He was thrilled to be here in fine fettle as each new December rolled around. I wanted to sleep from October until April.

Time, meditation and coming to my senses have helped lift that soggy blanket from my shoulders. While my energy and health, our fortunes, are not as they once were, our capacity for gladness seems robust. Since love is one of my year-round antidotes for sinking spells, along with beauty and music, I am aware of an even stronger urge to fling it far and wide, a continually thrown bride's bouquet, as the year closes.

We all become confused at times, forgetting that nothing is ever really as much about what we receive as what we give. Seeing familiar and difficult dates cycle back to us on the calendar does not mean they will batter us anew. That I am not 13 is no impediment to glimpsing, sensing the magic I've always connected to these days when night falls early and the nostalgic glow of Christmas lights (I could never decide which was my favorite color) keeps warm the dreams in our child hearts.

Tonic

The art of Cate Edwards revives me, it puts back together parts that have gone asunder. In her color, lines, shapes, patterns, figures, faces and wordless stories I regroup and find the world as I wish it to be. There are precarious rides, curious submergings and what appears to be considerable wild abandon, in the best, most life-affirming sense.

In the world away from images that support my soul, I find these to be dark and troubling times. It may be that times are always dark and troubling. What I know is my energy and a version of sanity are better served by stepping back from public debate. I choose not to express outrage through social media. I prefer to bring light of a sort. As a friend wisely wrote a day or so ago, art will not save us but it may cushion the fall. Art gives us everything it has, whether we create it or observe. Ghandi said, "Be the change you wish to see in the world." Right now, this is the way I can practice such advice.

I would love to be one of Cate Edwards' humans, to inhabit a flowered bowl, pose with my swimsuit-clad sisters near a pool or the sea, commune with other Earth creatures, continually surprised by the circumstance in which we find ourselves. Her work proves to me the connection between eyes and heart for as I scan her leaves and flowers, ornaments, marks and groupings, I have a physiological response, a quickened pulse, accompanied by a sense of longing. I want this to be our world.

Wobble

From 1940 until 1966, Pasadena was home of the Winter Garden, a vast-seeming, free-standing ice rink that briefly served as location for a live weekly music-and-ice-skating tv show called *Frosty Frolics.* That was around 1951. I think it must have run a bit longer than the one year, for I remember it, and *Your Hit Parade*, as family viewing. *Frosty Frolics* was likely the inspiration, however wrong-minded, for my one attempt at ice skating. Weak ankles, my neighbor and friend Susie Miller declared. That I went on, not too far into the future, to dance *en pointe* never quite erased the sense of failure brought on by ankles that wobbled. My very first time, yet my inability to achieve instant perfection kept me from trying again, even wanting to try again. I also never learned to ride a bicycle.

I am grateful to have survived childhood without any bullying that I can remember. I was capable of creating that sense of insufficiency unaided through harsh and unreasonable comparisons. Susie and I were sidewalk roller skating pals and I did not wobble on four wheels. I was solid and not accident prone. I was also timid about activities that seemed—and sometimes were—dangerous and felt myself shrink in stature as others plunged into new adventures. Unknown at that time was my future assignment as a contemplative. The things I couldn't do well mattered more than talents I couldn't name or understand. Had it not been for ballet, for dancing in general, for hopscotch, jump robe and being moderately okay at baseball, I would have been an elementary school dud. Dodge ball was scary and playground equipment (probably now against the law) like the rings, and bars (the dreaded "skin the cat," in which I hated being upside down), and such gave me the heebie-jeebies.

There is, I swear, something about emotions that accompany the onset of Christmas that bring up memories, welcome or not. For the moment I trust that these thoughts of, if not humiliation, then certainly not triumph have come to be acknowledged and released. They've been taking up shelf space for far too long. I still wobble, only now I wobble better. I have become the definition of wobbling.

Ardent

It is the Solstice night as I write this, time of the new moon, beginning of the return of the light. We have been reminded throughout the day about setting our minds to new ways of being, of doing. If we remain or become ardent, how can we go wrong. Ardent, fervent, passionate. Aflame, unbounded, electric, aglow, burning.

Music and musicians, color and color and color. Tepid is not the temperature we require to carry us across winter's dark expanse. *Caliente*, all spice and tang, flavor and, again, color. We cannot find our way by candles too dim. What we need is emphatic, even extreme. We will not melt our own frozen beliefs without turning up the heat. Our rigid joints will not loosen without a glow that matches the sun.

On the longest night of the year, even Los Angeles yearns for a hearth with warming flames. Heat in its dazzling manifestations expands us, will not let us shrink nor be less than we are.

Aspire

I find hope to be a sturdy, inspirational tool. I believe that pretty much anything can happen, including impossible things, and what I may not be doing or creating today is no indicator of what I may be capable of tomorrow, or even later this afternoon. What do they say? It is never too late to become who you might have been. I aspire to reach beyond this moment, in ways imagined as well as unimaginable, while simultaneously learning to be content with what is. We are all contortionists in training, planted in the present, extending our vines toward the future.

A unicycle rider on a tightrope is no less challenged by balance than any earthbound dreamer. How do we savor contentment with now, full of gratitude, while still reaching for more. We plot, sketch, envision, write lists, make wishes and, in my case, inch ahead with a new medium, an unfamiliar form of expression. It may be age, it may be caution, it may be fatigue which causes me to proceed slowly, regardless of the heat generated by enthusiasm. From here I can see where I'd like to be, see what the finished work looks like, yet how it feels is that in order to get there I first have to machete a path through the undergrowth, clear a campsite and then with a stilled mind set to the task. Knowing that I am the thorny shrubs through which I must navigate does not make it any easier. There is more peace-making to be done, more compassion required, certainly more patience. I will always be the child who grows more stubborn when jerked by the arm.

When observing or reading of others' forward sprints, it is a challenge not to compare, an act which invariably finds me finishing well out of the money. We late bloomers, I hope one day to be their poster child, awaken, arise and advance in a fashion that often draws eye rolls and sighs of exasperation from those of swifter foot. Hope and aspiration are companions for the long haul. We are comfortable sitting in occasional silence, quietly cheering the sun across the sky, knowing the road goes on forever.

Nancy Drew

As a girl I often spent the days following Christmas or my birthday devouring the Nancy Drew books I received as gifts. In those days the Pasadena Library System felt such pulp was beneath their dignity and did not carry Nancy or any other popular, and apparently trashy, series. Ownership and trading was our only option.

Then last week Lisa Hoffman, an adventurous and reliable source for stuff I don't know about, mentioned the luminous Essie Davis, her homegrown horror film, *The Babadook*, and Australian tv series, *Miss Fisher Mysteries.* Netflix-available, we began watching with Season One, Episode One that night. I enjoy the programs just as I did those blue-bound volumes so very many years ago.

Set in the 1920s with lavish fashion, interiors and vehicles that let you know where you are without feeling like a documentary, each story took me back to the scenes of earlier crimes, as I had started reading Nancy before she was modernized. My girl detective drove a roadster and appeared on the colorful dust jackets in sensible yet stylish garb of an era very close to the flapper age. Miss Fisher is, of course, more mature and considerably less chaste than Miss Drew (my son's frame of reference was Veronica Mars) and all the more appealing for it.

Even though I've managed to find a low-key footpath through Christmas, I still experience a bit of let-down when the chocolate gobbling has to stop and it seems that one needs to resume some version of regular life. Miss Fisher adds the right amount of fizz to an outlook grown a bit too flat. It was also abnormally cold for Southern California this past week. At least we in the San Gabriel Valley didn't have snow in our yards though there was frost on the roofs. Any tolerance I once had for cold has vanished (how lucky

I live in Los Angeles and not Billings, Montana) and I find myself longing for summer which is still but a distant hope. Without central heat, this is the land of many layers and of following the southern sunlight as though I were producing cholorophyll.

We have the return of *Downton Abbey* and *The Good Wife* to help see us through any January doldrums. As they have been joined by the handsomely-crafted Australian mysteries we may, with the addition of rededicating several hours a day to writing and drawing, find a crumb-trail back to warmer days (my mind may be trying to hibernate) without a complete loss of zest. Nancy Drew always was a favorite winter chum.

Il a plu—it rained

Saturday's not entirely expected day-long showers made working on two illustrated envelopes that much more jolly. I cannot think when last my deadline converged with conditions that matched what I used to count on from January and February. These were commissioned birthday envelopes, drawing and pencil coloring.

When I was finished and had time to think about it, the day reminded me of making or addressing valentines. Shiny red heart stickers from Mrs. Grossman or cut-out-and-paste envelopes from a book of punch-out cards for classmates, manipulated under light from the dining room chandelier, that's perfect work for a drizzling Saturday.

I chose French for the words this week, for it is now Sunday and news stories say more than 3,000,000 have gathered in Paris for a unity march. And Gene Kelly is equal parts *An American in Paris* and *Singing In the Rain.* Further convergence.

It is still raining, in spurts and waves, as Sunday noon approaches. The envelopes have been delivered, an assignment completed. Peace and contentment are not distant dreams, they are readily, easily, at hand. All that is asked of us is to remain open to new definitions of what is enough.

Exterior

The process of maturing, evolving (one hopes), becoming, is interior. There have been moments of craving a muffler-length flowered cotton scarf, rose patterned socks or a red lipstick but mostly it has been about shedding outworn beliefs, acknowledging that nothing is guaranteed and adapting to the world as it is.

Comes a time, though, when redecorating one's exterior begins to appeal, almost to the point of obsession. Thanks (I believe that would be the accurate word) to Pinterest, I have found what I want to be my style in these advancing years. The means to make that possible have not yet appeared. I am not discouraged.

As with so many aspects of human life, I feel a time machine would be a useful device to (a) return to the easier availability of luxury fabrics close to home and (b) obtain them at their 1970s, if not earlier, prices. Once you've seen an outfit in silk, anything that is not silk seems a poor second choice. This all sounds, I realize, embarrassingly trivial, especially when positioned next to aspects of reality that keep us all awake at night. That alone is reason enough to spend fantasy time imagining one's self as stunning for no reason or occasion. The world will not set itself aright because I stop mooning over clothes I wish I'd seen 40 years ago. I used to sew reasonably well. I might be able to do it again.

The point of this is to be a bit silly. In the first place, we like what we like, we love what we love and it is unkind to the point of sadism to curtail harmless daydreaming. Just as with actual children, we know better than to yank our interior child selves by the arm, scowl and drag us out of the store, ashamed, yet not understanding why. It has become part of my manifesto, the belief that beauty as we identify it feeds our hearts and souls.

Beauty makes us strong, even though we can grow weak at the knees in its presence. Shame and a sense of lack deplete us, tarnish what glows from within and without. To link arms with beauty does not require possessing its coveted manifestations. Sometimes to imagine is enough.

Harken

Usually what we love has been what we loved since childhood, or nearly. Pinterest allows me to harken back to fashion inspiration from the 1950s, particularly anything involving net or tulle. Once we wore petticoats.

My influence is not just from, as they were sometimes called, crinolines, but also a lavender ballet dress my mother made for a recital. Being one of the older and taller students at the Metcalf School of Ballet and Tap, my gown was "ballet" length, defined as mid-calf or just above the ankle. I have no idea how many layers went into the skirt, only that they were multiple. It floated, twirled and seemed the epitome of grace. In contrast, petticoats had to be starched regularly. Without starching they wouldn't have pouffed our skirts out to *there* but instead just hung inert from their elastic waists making us look bulky instead of cute. Cute was the bullseye at which we all, boys and girls, aimed.

Until they went out of fashion, perhaps around 1960, I used to starch my petticoats in a galvanized washtub on the driveway. Once starched, each had to be dried, usually clipped to a skirt or pants hanger, suspended from something in the garage. When dry, they could stand on their own. I believe my usual number of them was three. Eventually they grew too old to hold a starching so they either had to be replaced or added to. I bought them with my allowance at the W. T. Grant dimestore in downtown Pasadena. They had the best prices.

Pinterest enlightened me about tulle skirts as appropriate outerwear. The fact that I haven't yet joined this trend doesn't mean I won't. With encouragement from *Advanced Style*, we *women of a certain age* find it possible to consider fashion choices to which, at times not so long past, no harkening would have been allowed.

That the skirts are often shown topped by what could have been the height of bad-girl style in the late '50s, a cardigan sweater buttoned up the back(!), makes it feel like *deja vu*, as though I'd left the house without a real skirt over the petticoats.

Those things which please or entice us most seem to be etched onto our hearts. Anything from playing with puppets to keeping track of things in pocket-sized notebooks or hyperventilating over frothy yard goods gives us dimension, authenticity, and honors early passions. It is not nostalgia, it is consistency.

Reconnaissance

There are some things that cannot be *reconnoitered.* Such as the future, our futures, what comes next. Even with the most imaginative homemade device we will not be able to see around that particular corner.

In another lifetime I consulted psychics, astrologers. I thought they could, for varying fees, apply their periscopes to my unseen destiny and assure me that all I hoped for would come to pass. Eventually I realized it was just so much piffle. They couldn't tell me and I no longer wanted to know.

It is not difficult to envision that most of us are familiar with expanses, jagged and bleak, from which we'd rather escape. What better destination than a promised tomorrow where all is bliss. I know addiction, dissociation, torpor, depression and despair. The great miracle is that they are no longer chronic states. Their shadowy overhang once kept sunlight from the garden. That is different now.

Time and love, that of self and others, carry us beyond our grimmest days. It is work and it is worth it. As much as I craved the assurance of peace to come, I would never have believed anyone who described this path to me. Or maybe they did and because it seemed so unlikely I simply forgot. As it feels the most accurate name for them, I swear there are angels, fierce angels, who take up our cause, especially when it feels lost. Once we recognize all life as an act of faith, we become our own seers.

Valentine

With or without a traditional *sweetheart*, I am a fool for Valentine's Day and its message, "Send Love."

The trappings, of course, speak directly to my child and grown-up soul: paper, red, ribbons, doilies, stickers, handmade cards and envelopes and hearts, miles and miles of hearts.

I have come through the softening effects of time to know that love is the infrastructure of existence. It is, in the ideal, who we are meant to be, what we are here to do. While there are so many variations of its expression, I consider sharing to be the top choice. It is the jolliest potluck we will ever attend, the one at which whatever we have and bring is enough.

We get to be the chocolate covered marshmallow candy, squishable, thin of shell. We have the option to reach much more than halfway, to reach ALL the way to connect with anyone, everyone. It is not about what we get but what we give. Let us listen to what intuition confides and act upon it. There is infinite space within our human hearts.

We are asked to be patient with what we see as our shortcomings, asked to love ourselves out of the belief that we are lacking. We are the raw materials through which change comes into the world, one kind or encouraging or inspiring word at a time. We are a source of magic, of beauty, of wonder, part of nature, blessed with the gift of language and the power to heal. We are, oh the impossible luck, the Valentines.

Makers

Bakers bake, builders build, crafters craft. We are all makers of something. We are, in fact, alchemists, taking raw materials and transforming them into something entirely new and different. It is magic, pure and true.

Every meal cooked is a creative act, as is every sentence written. Makers are midwives, attendants, facilitators, as one form becomes another.

Because life is serial problem-solving, we may grow away from noticing and claiming our inventiveness. I love the image of unmatched socks, assuming the knitter had tons of short leftover bits which could not be turned into an identical pair, except perhaps for a newborn, and had to improvise. With a beautiful result.

We put together, we invent, we make do, make it up, reclaim, repurpose and possibly forget all those resume-worthy acts. Skills, Napoleon Dynamite said, "Girls only want boyfriends who have great skills." Do not underestimate yourself in the skills department. You're welcome.

Seasonal

My childhood memory of February skies displays them as cloudy. After two weeks of sunshine and some record temperatures, Saturday morning arrived with a more expectedly seasonal overcast and Sunday the same. Rain in the afternoon, rain heavy enough to hear which is not always the case.

Within the past few weeks two friends mentioned keeping notebooks of how they spend their days. One has maintained this activity since 1984. I find such consistency admirable, enviable and so far outside my experience that considering it leaves me bewildered. I think if I kept such a record, assuming I noted the weather for each day, which would be a simple task, a few words, I would know just what the sky was doing on a specific February day. I even ordered a notebook similar to one a friend described, attracted to her vertical format for listing bullet points. The book arrived a week ago. Getting in the habit of using it challenges me and using it with flair and color and creativity, as she does, feels like trying to teach myself Mandarin.

A shared Facebook post from *The Marginalian* offered Mary Oliver talking about habit. It is an article I need to read more than once, allowing time for a good soaking-in.

> *What some might call the restrictions of the daily office they find to be an opportunity to foster the inner life. The hours are appointed and named . . . Life's fretfulness is transcended. The different and the novel are sweet, but regularity and repetition are also teachers . . . And if you have no ceremony, no habits, which may be opulent or may be simple but are exact and rigorous and familiar, how can you reach toward the actuality of faith, or even a moral life, except vaguely? The patterns of our lives reveal us. Our*

habits measure us. Our battles with our habits speak of dreams yet to become real.

What is habit if not a practice of consistency or a dedication to it, intentional or not. I think about being consistent, which I equate with being reliable, as one of the hurdles that confronts me. It has a lot of company. A daily jotting of words or phrases to preserve time seems an especially worthy habit. I trust it is one I can learn.

Contain

Do I contradict myself? Very well, then I contradict myself,
I am large, I contain multitudes.

— Walt Whitman

The word "contain" takes me in so many directions. At first I thought of the likelihood that others who fancy pens and notebooks, as I do, are also drawn to things that hold other things. If we have pencils, we need a pencil box. If we have color pencils, we need an array of easy-to-access storage in which to sort them into color families, types, manufacturers. There is pleasure, for some of us, in winnowing them into smaller and smaller categories, like biological classifications: class, order, genus, species, and variety.

Then I thought, "I can't contain myself," to describe a state of such heightened excitement that we start to overflow our banks. Containing one's self or the attempt to do so may fall into the category of overrated actions. I have probably mentioned before my aunt's comment when asked about a comedy film she'd just seen. "It was so funny I could hardly keep from laughing." Decorum. I'm not so sure.

Among us pen types, I suspect that old luggage is a favorite, right up there with cigar boxes. It is the odd but not uncommon heart which rejoices at a stack of vintage suitcases. And where else to keep real treasures but a cigar box. Literature supports this truth.

I like hard copies of things, an address book full of crossed-out, rewritten entries, scrap paper notes, torn envelopes, held closed with a rubber band. Because my father kept files of things like clippings, correspondence, carbons of his stories, I am lured by file folders and file cabinets. I grew to adulthood working in offices, filing. The emphatic sound of a metal file draw sliding shut will never be mistaken for anything else.

I have tried, without success, even consulting my poetry angel, to find the source of a poem I *think* I remember from a high school or junior college class in the '60s about how bag people go looking for bags, box people go looking for boxes. Having fallen short of that goal, here is a bit more Whitman, wiser than many men. I think this is so lovely. Contained by time.

We were together. I forget the rest.

— Walt Whitman

Missive

I once sent a dozen of my friends a telegram saying 'flee at once—all is discovered.' They all left town immediately.

— Mark Twain
(also attributed to Sir Arthur Conan Doyle)

I'm sticking with the pre-computer definition of missive as a frequently handwritten note or bit of communication, not an email or text. As wildly passionate as I am about typewriters, I suppose it is my own narrow thinking that seeks penmanship. We can leave the debate open on that. Dictionaries differ on the content of a missive—some say lengthy , others say brief, urgent—and remain, shall we say, flexible about the handwritten requirement.

Picture the cardboard rectangle that arrives with a bouquet of flowers or a tiny folded card with room for just a few meaningful words. These are mementos to be saved, perhaps even glued into a baby book.

On the occasion of her birthday this past week, an artist friend shared a handwritten note from her father, telling her of his feelings on the day she was born. Reading it made me wish, as do many things, that I'd saved every loving, cheering missive I'd ever received. To have not just the good wishes or sincere feelings of those we've loved but their distinctive handwriting as well, what a treasure.

Asking myself why, with such a fondness for pens and papers, I send so few pieces of real snail mail, I have only one answer. Inertia. I am a reasonable email correspondent or sender of Facebook messages. A letter IS a letter. Electronics do not render it invalid or inferior. Still.

As proof that I am not the only one presently concerned with missives and their importance in our lives, here are some projects and/or products that are able defense witnesses.

At *Letters of Note*, Shaun Usher is at work on Volume II of collected correspondence. Among the "most fascinating" letters on the blog is this, excerpted, from John Steinbeck to his eldest son:

> *If you love someone—there is no possible harm in saying so—only you must remember that some people are very shy and sometimes the saying must take that shyness into consideration.*
>
> *Girls have a way of knowing or feeling what you feel, but they usually like to hear it also.*
>
> *It sometimes happens that what you feel is not returned for one reason or another—but that does not make your feeling less valuable and good.*
>
> *Lastly, I know your feeling because I have it and I'm glad you have it.*
>
> *We will be glad to meet Susan. She will be very welcome. But Elaine will make all such arrangements because that is her province and she will be very glad to. She knows about love too and maybe she can give you more help than I can.*
>
> *And don't worry about losing. If it is right, it happens—The main thing is not to hurry. Nothing good gets away.*
>
> *Love,*
> *Fa*

A visit to the Post Office or usps.com for colorful forever postage stamps will help speed your missives on their way.

Willing suspension of disbelief

Meaning

The temporary acceptance as believable of events or characters that would ordinarily be seen as incredible. This is usually to allow an audience to appreciate works of literature or drama that are exploring unusual ideas.

Origin

This term was coined by Samuel Taylor Coleridge in 1817 with the publication of his *Biographia literaria or biographical sketches of my literary life and opinions*:

> *In this idea originated the plan of the 'Lyrical Ballads'; in which it was agreed, that my endeavours should be directed to persons and characters supernatural, or at least romantic, yet so as to transfer from our inward nature a human interest and a semblance of truth sufficient to procure for these shadows of imagination that willing suspension of disbelief for the moment, which constitutes poetic faith.*

The state is arguably an essential element when experiencing any drama or work of fiction. We may know very well that we are watching an actor or looking at marks on paper, but we wilfully accept them as real in order to fully experience what the artist is attempting to convey.

Poetic faith. A good story is a good story.

Over the weekend we watched *Interstellar* (directed by Christopher Nolan, written by Christopher Nolan and Jonathan Nolan) which I've since learned opened to very mixed reviews.

I loved it, was so deeply in its thrall that my frequently twitching legs were still for nearly three hours. My mind never wandered, my eyes never left the screen. When the last credit had rolled by, my son said he wished he'd seen it in IMAX format, though our home tv did not disappoint in any way.

I have no intention of deconstructing the movie to, if it were possible, discover why my poetic faith was so intense. That fact that the science involved was so far beyond my ability to comprehend, I could not possibly scoff at any theories put forth. Mostly, it was the humanity of the characters that held my attention and belief. They expressed a version of humanity sometimes missing in science fiction, which is no deterrent to my enjoyment of the genre. It made identifying with them in their extreme circumstances so much easier.

Staying away from chat rooms in which rancor seems to be the over-riding tone is near the top of my list for how to remain relatively sane. My son, younger and more resilient, will visit them, read so much utter drivel that he begins to rant and thus has information about what bizarre opinions are expressed on any and every topic. I have very old-fashioned views about what ought to be allowed into the collective dialogue and what should not. I feel strongly that we get to enjoy, even to love, what pleases us, without explanation or challenge. That my feelings are not universally shared is fine, it's expected. All I ask is to be left in peace with my choices.

Whether from cranks or experts, I prefer not to hear about all that is wrong with a story that has touched me. We choose to suspend disbelief in our own ways. Without spoiling the plot of *Interstellar*, I will just say that to the best of my knowledge no human has experienced a black hole. We can only theorize, as in guess, how they behave.

Some reviewers called the movie cold. It felt anything but cold to me. For science fiction, it seemed quite warm-blooded. The real issue, though, is that a writer gets to tell his or her story. We either buy into it or we don't. I have a number of sci-fi movie favorites, including *Blade Runner, Close Encounters, Aliens, Star Wars* (or is that even considered science fiction?) and many others in print form. I grew up on Ray Bradbury.

What I enjoy is being transported, taken from ordinary reality and everyday concerns to a place where the circumstances are far removed yet not unfamiliar. There are multiple sites where you can read either reviews of *Interstellar* or a synopsis of its plot. If you decide to watch, you will likely know before too many minutes have passed whether or not you can accept the premise, the characters and their plight as real or not. Fiction, film or print, gives us vicarious lives to live for short spans, though the memories of those adventures can remain with us for decades. The measure of a great story is our ability to inhabit it fully, whether in this world or another.

Part IV

Mull

How is a thought like an iceberg? Ponder, contemplate, consider, weigh, think. Good thing I'm not a zealot for quantifying. I don't want to know how much of any day I spend asking myself rhetorical questions, posing conundrums, seeking answers where perhaps none exist. It is not time wasted, however. If we don't *wonder* about *things*, we are marooned. Mulling gives us bearings or at least tells us where we are not.

"My apologies to great questions for small answers." From her poem "Under One Small Star" by Wislawa Szymborska.

The moon often appears, or plays a leading role, in the art of Quint Buchholz. The moon is an attractive object for mullers. Mystery is attractive to mullers, or more accurately, is essential. If we knew the secrets we would have no need to ask the questions.

To mull is not to deconstruct (shudder). If I arrive at any truths, ever, it is by widening the screen, not narrowing my focus. It seems to be a process of allowing rather than intention, clearing space on a shelf then leaving the room to see what comes to settle in the empty spot. Mulling, contemplation generally, is similar to my approach to writing fiction. I stand at the curb waiting for a car to pull up, then watch to see who gets out.

Rilke told us to love and to live the questions. Do not forget that being comfortable with not knowing isn't the same as not asking.

Imperfect

My maternal grandmother had an expression, "It isn't Boston but it IS Massachusetts." I have used it hundreds of times to describe why what may seem second best is not so far from being just right.

Consider this: if perfection existed, we'd never have learned how to make-do. Aren't you just a little bit pleased with all the problems you've solved, all the crises you've mended, by finding the second, third or fifteenth good-as-perfect way to make things come out?

Life is filled with circumstances guaranteed to make the sane turn crazy and cause the crazy to combust spontaneously. The more relaxed, the less invested we can be about the means and the end, the happier we are likely to remain.

The fact that we prefer a thing to be a certain way does not mean ours is the only answer. Absolutes do not appear often in matters of, say, arranging spices on the kitchen shelves. Collectively, we confuse "preferred" with "right," i.e. perfect. Nay, I say.

In much younger and massively less enlightened days, I thought to myself of my then-husband, "If you loved me, you'd take out the trash NOW." Good luck with that, we see how IT turned out.

It is not just about making peace with what is, though that is part of the equation. This existence is not the *Good Will Hunting* math problem with one, only one, solution. (I use a movie reference for my own math experience stopped long before reaching such a plateau.) There are so many ways of being right, or at least of being adequate, workable, acceptable and okay.

Imperfect is an opportunity to find another answer. As we celebrate so many things we love in April, poetry, letter writing, libraries, why not add imperfection to the list. It isn't going to go away. It truly is the thing that wouldn't leave. Let's try to pretend that we love it until we really can.

Red

I left you notes on pages from old ledgers, tucked into manilla coin envelopes with your name, "Red," written with a brush-tip pen after practicing over and over, getting the lines just thin enough *here,* thick enough *there* so it mimicked Copperplate which I haven't quite had time to master.

The correspondence couldn't be called anything but mash notes, professions of love from the moonstruck, the spellbound, the captivated fan. We couldn't date in any usual sense though I would be so proud to escort any of your manifestations anywhere. I've worn you as a scarf, a zippered and hooded sweater, ballet flats, a Norma Kamali shirtwaist with shoulder pads and side-seam pockets. You've become my favorite shade of lipstick and I'd still choose you for lingerie, just another eccentricity. My response is Pavlovian when I see you in a painting not seen before, in a newly-designed couture gown, in exotic textiles. You make me want a pair of Converse hi-tops and the shorty coat I had in 1963, the one with big buttons and deep patch pockets. For you I would wear nail polish.

Because of you, mostly, Valentine's Day remains a dreamy holiday. Red roses rock, ditto cinnamon red hots. Without you, romance would be a sad, pallid business. Dear Red, Do you even know how hot you are? Sound of sizzling, followed by a tango.

Mixtape

Not sure what they call them anymore since we, meaning they, don't use cassettes. I still prefer CD to digital and I still have mixtapes from decades ago and they haven't (or hadn't) lost their shape or sound. I also continue to believe that a mixtape is an accurate representation of (a) the moment, (b) a very finite number of our favorite songs or (c) our ability to use other people's words to deliver our message. For my (b), the problem if there was one would be how to keep it from being Van Morrison-heavy.

To be known, is there any part of life less easily conquered? First to be known to ourselves, not confused nor self-deceiving, then to find the means of communicating that, either by living it, writing it, speaking it, acting it out in pantomime, to significant others. Our human ability to misconstrue is without limit, as though existence were a *cinema noir* classic in which we each play a protagonist of limited vision who only dreams of the big score. Yes, I have recently been watching and thinking about *noir.* I can tell you this, the cartel always wins.

With the discovery of Pinterest, I found knitting artists who produce non-matching socks by the pair. They are jewels for the feet, rare and beautiful and, it seems, frequently made from last small bits of yarn leftover from other projects. I know I am one of those pair, not one row like another, disparate parts scattered all over the landscape. I believe most of us are. Our songs will be as divergent as our thoughts and favorite foods. A mixtape can be the microcosm, the linear presentation of peaks and valleys, a map of preferences in a way the brain can process it, us as a medley of our greatest hits which we feel no compulsion to explain.

Rewrite

A rewrite is as good as a do-over. It gives a nod of assent to changing our mind. Oh, yes, this IS better than that.

Perception may be 100% of any situation, which becomes something new when we can see it differently. Anxiety is the lurking vortex, not quite invisible from the corner of the eye, its loud slurping reminding that fear and worry, even despair are always available choices. We don't have to take that road.

Sunday morning, ordinary life challenges, the option of lapsing into hand-wringing and full-on dither. Or, finding a way to do what absolutely has to be done in the moment and simply assuming that all will be well. Not my job to know how, my only job is to trust, listen to what wisdom guides me and be honestly cheerful. There have been countless challenges and I'm still here

Nor can we change the past, only the way we view it. Even if it has felt like a nightmare for decades, responsible, or so we imagine, for ruining our lives, we can assign it a new role, reinterpret its influence, thank it for the unlikely gift of helping us become who we are. Darkness and pain are not what the universe of my understanding wishes for me, though I haven't always known that. Illumination, gratitude, peace and joy are what I prefer. Raise your copy pencils, change the story. We are not too old to learn new tricks.

Everyday

Holiness comes wrapped in the ordinary.
There are burning bushes all around you.
Every tree is full of angels.
Hidden beauty is waiting in every crumb.

— Macrina Wiederkehr

Each morning brings a new voyage, the destination always unknown. Our lives are packed full as vacation suitcases with the everyday, from which the chance for miracles, for wonders, always arises.

In some now-dim past as I began my first gratitude journal, I realized that "I'm still here" was a significant declaration, not some ho-hum, I've run out of things to say, default. It is not so much that peril just lurks, loiters, expecting our unwariness. It is more that the unforeseen, the unwelcome, finds us all. I celebrate surviving those encounters. Best not to take them at face value for frequently it is within them that we see the impossible manifest.

Whether I feel equal to the task or pitiful and outnumbered, life seems to expect me to show up every day. I suspect one of the attractions I feel for the color red is its boldness. Red does not cower or apologize for being. It does not explain, simply bringing as much glorious redness as it can muster to circumstances of the moment. We don't notice its flattened hair, pouchy eyes or abbreviated attention span. It may appear wearing house pants and pilly socks. No matter what, it is still red and it is here, at its heart always and only red. Why would we be different?

We, you and I, are pieces of holiness that come wrapped in the ordinary. Even when we can't claim to be fully robust with optimism, with enviable efficiency or even physical strength, we remain seers, questing souls, our hues authentically bright. Because we know it exists, hidden beauty is the source of our secret strength.

Invent

Even the most able-bodied among us has a need to adapt from time to time. When one door closes, turn around and go the other way. If a possibility has been exhausted, invent or discover a new option. It is a form of mental duct tape, putting pieces together that have been rent asunder. Making things work.

As you may already know, Henri Matisse, no longer able to paint or draw as he once had, turned to a giant pair of shears, gouache-painted papers and cut-out shapes to make art for an album called *Jazz*.

Making things work, whatever the things, allows us to feel, to be, undefeated. Having only a Plan A for any situation leaves no escape hatch. I believe strongly that very little in our human existence has only one right answer. We develop a vocabulary of second chances: adapt, adjust, reconsider, improvise, redefine, wing it. Cooking offers itself as a model for such behavior. We are greater than a mostly-bare cupboard. We will prevail, there will be dinner and it will taste good.

It is not scientific but in my experience there is always a way. *Some* way. The molecules of the situation may have to be rearranged to create an original life form and so what? We build new neural pathways with just this sort of problem-solving.

Grab those enormous scissors and change the shape of what it ought to be to what it CAN be. The genius of Henri Matisse will light the way.

Adrift

Things unroll, misalign, fall, elude and, sometimes, vanish. Wobble-free steadiness seems too much to ask. There we are, no longer properly moored, having trouble surrendering the need for an immediate solution. Wonky seems to be one of my constants.

In my family there was a long-discussed wool plaid picnic blanket that eventually came to me. Unremarkable in all respects, other than being mended with silver duct tape, its appeal must have been too subtle for my sensibilities. It was too pointlessly, needlessly wonky. I said, no thank you. No one remains to ask about this curiosity. I only just remembered the fact of it.

It is, literally and metaphorically, about getting the holes to line up. One part of life can't be affixed to another if the phillips head screws are not a straight fit. Even if the day itself has askew portions, the feeling of things gone-out-of-true is within. It is uncomfortable and generally unfixable. Oh, dandy, I think, another warty booger to befriend.

For however long I am separated from my shore, my actually reliable center, I twitch and squirm. Vague and momentary pains jostle my legs. Focus wants to trade places with sleep. Eyes and mind wander. And I know that just as suddenly as this flux state overtook me it will depart. Bobbing corks on an endless sea.

Legacy

John Ford is the only director who has won four Best Director Academy Awards. His legacy, in which he is called variously one of the top three directors ever or, by Orson Welles, the best, is enviable, defies challenge and endures. It is said that regardless of where his westerns were set, he filmed them in Monument Valley. It is land that I will always associate with him, as though he gave it voice.

Any of us who make things—poems, stories, movies, art, meals—must secretly harbor at least a faint wish that some of our efforts live after us. My maternal grandmother was not an artist in a professional sense, yet it was her recipes for tamale pie and rice pudding that I wanted served at my wedding. My late cousin and I learned as girls to make her Cornish pasties. If my son can be lured away from his Mexican and Asian dishes, perhaps he can be the next pasty generation.

As I write this on Father's Day, I think of the body of work my father created and how it still breathes. A younger writer with whom he became friends has taken on the task, to which he seems most dedicated, of compiling Dad's biography, including decades of newspaper columns, magazine articles, children's books and, especially, books about car travel throughout California. The author has shared facts with me that I never knew. I can't say it is immortality, for who knows how long any of our species will be here on this warming planet (Werner Herzog is not optimistic), yet the words Dad wrote, the immeasurable time spent in research and interview, contributed to material with lasting value. He has become, in his way, part of California history, recounting and, by doing so, preserving.

He also left his three children with a model of caring deeply about California's ancient trees and desert lands, native people, about the precision of words. We lived and watched as he practiced his craft, utilized his gifts, established solid professional footing. It was not a democracy, our childhood home, and the wide shadow he cast likely left indelible marks. Still, we became soft in ways we had not witnessed, soft meaning willing to adapt, to surrender to what could not be changed. We learned to find and revere what spoke to our hearts, to do our best to see that certain values were honored, elevated. We know that unnameable parts of us, parts of which we have become fond, would not exist had our raising been different. Legacy is a shape-shifter, coyote one moment, spirit guide the next, variable as fog off the rocky coast of Big Sur. Through intention or chance, we leave our mark. Legacy means we remain.

West

Lucky me, I didn't have to come west. I was already here.

As children about three years old, both of my parents moved to Southern California with their families, my father from Illinois, my mother from Michigan. Both families chose the midwestern sensibility of Pasadena, though my father, uncle and grandparents eventually settled on a farm in the San Joaquin Valley. My best guess is that it more nearly matched the life my grandfather knew. My parents met during World War II while attending the University of New Mexico at Albuquerque, Mother working toward her BFA, Father there as part of his Navy Officer Candidate School. My brother, sister and I were all born in Pasadena.

Until I heard Lucinda Williams sing *West,* I'd forgotten that my former and late husband, growing up in South Africa with western dreams fueled by his Yankee father and Hollywood depictions, was determined to reach California. Newspaper work knows no geographical limits and he believed there would always be employment wherever he landed. After reporting jobs in Virginia and New Jersey, after Army service at Ft. Knox, after the Associated Press, he claimed the West as home. Though Lucinda's West is not California, it is close enough in spirit and allure. I think it's a swell song.

Notes

Notes, as in take them copiously. Notes, as in jot it down. Notes, as in handwritten. To keep them in any form is an encouraging first step. To take them in some orderly fashion so that I may find them again is the ideal. My life and I are works in progress.

A shared article from the *NY Times* about what we lose as we lose handwriting reminded me that I do exercise penmanship every day. A good thing, as fond as I am of pens. A better thing for it seems to keep aspects of the brain engaged in a way that using a keyboard does not. I suspect (or may have read, too) that doodling is also good for us in a similar way.

I see the hand as a loyal family retainer of the old school, taking up the pen or pencil in a last stand for civilization in the face of chaos. Yet recently fresh recruits have appeared on the horizon, a younger generation who have sworn allegiance to what they call analog. They are keepers of notebooks and planners, purchasers of fountain pens with triple-digit prices, sketchers and defenders of the high art of hand lettering, inventors of fonts and illustrators of life's often mundane interludes. They may be the new radicals, owners of iPhones, of tablets, who keep track of what matters by writing it down on paper.

For years I've known that I am more likely to remember something when my hand plays a part in preserving it. Under optimal circumstances I may even recall where on the page I wrote it, the name of the poet or illustrator or blogger, squeezed between a reminder to "Visualize Today" and encouragement to "Respond to all areas of your life with love and kindness."

Cloudy

Sunshine dulls the mind to risk and thoughtfulness.

The brilliant and indefatigable Maria Popova of *The Marginalian* shared why cloudy days help us think more clearly.

I have my own anecdotal experience of clear skies vs. cloudy skies, nothing to do with cognitive improvement, or maybe it is, but very much to do with a sense of comfort and safety. In a lengthy period of slow recovery from pneumonia resulting in chronic respiratory infections and a diagnosis of chronic fatigue, I found that an overcast sky gave me a feeling of being enfolded, wrapped in what seemed a vast security blanket. I only noticed this when blue skies appeared, wide open, without limit, infinite, and how exposed and unsafe I felt.

How long it took to shake this dread of unobscured blue skies I can't recall, possibly a couple years. It was a sense of there being nothing between me and everything, between me and distant planets, the unknown reaches of space, the void. Cloudy brought comfort, as though someone had wisely thought to close the wide-open doors.

In thinking of this some 20 years after the fact, gray skies felt like permission to huddle and hunker, to go slowly, really, to hide. With clear, open skies came a feeling of expectation for which I wasn't ready. I still needed the cave, the small space in which I could touch all the walls. A sky that went on forever was too frightening. I remembered the nurse showing me how to wrap my newborn son tightly in his flannel blanket, saying babies felt unsafe when their limbs were allowed to wave about. For a time, knowing those blue skies reached into an unrestricted universe was more than I could bear.

I have come to love watching the sky from my second-floor windows, its drifting clouds, thick muffling of fog or, as today, limitlessness. Los Angeles is no place for a blue-sky phobia.

The Seven Myths of Mediation may help to assure you, as they did me, that imperfection of practice is no obstacle to meditating. In each of the sessions, led by Deepak Chopra with a mantra to repeat as a means of focusing, I have found an almost instant stilling of the chattering mind and a sense of what I assume to be the grace of which he and program partner Oprah Winfrey speak. That the road to this enlightened space is through gratitude makes it a good match for me. I have so much for which to be thankful and my days include conscious expression of gratitude for all things, to the best of my ability.

In discussing the Seven Myths, Chopra speaks of working with a trained teacher to learn the practice of meditation, something which had me believing I was doing it wrong (!) as I had only the teachings of CDs and books before finding these courses. I know people who have nearly life-long meditation practices which seem to ask more of them than I can give, being unable to sit in uncomfortable positions as my legs no longer bend that way, yet to find the quiet mind and optimism that I have here seems to tell me, as with so many things, we start where we are with what we have and do the best we can. Chopra is an excellent guide and teacher.

Unless one has already developed a rare sense of peace and stillness, the world is too much with us most of the time. In these roughly 20-minute sessions I become unknotted, calmed and restored, as in made more whole again. There is nothing to sell here, only a gift to bestow. In this practice or another which better suits your needs, meditation offers a respite from overload and my own tendency at times to become a bit wound up, to forget what I know and lapse into jabbering. It is lovely not to be jabbering, either out loud or in my own head. Surely that is grace.

Ballast

Not just for ships or hot air balloons, ballast, generally, is that which gives stability. For me that means sleep of a deep and dreaming sort. It means ample quiet, not doing more than one thing at a time if I can help it, an absence of chaos, remembering how many reasons I have to be grateful. It means love and kindness among family, friends and people I don't yet know well. It is slow and glad, it smiles at beauty and humor. It can no longer tolerate exchanges which lack harmony. It rejoices at good news, weeps when sad and wishes sugar wasn't so seductive.

My ballast, my stability is solid in its softness. Patience with all I could find to criticize about myself may seem a curious stability. It is ballast in the most basic definition: it keeps me on an even keel. I begin to hiss and spark when I take up dissatisfaction with my essential being. Finding fault with self or another is the unbalanced load in the old washing machine. The shrill whine and thudding can be heard all over the neighborhood.

It smells like freesias or the older vintage scent *Femme* or fresh mint. It tastes like iced decaf mocha or a perfectly ripe mango. The soul is shored up with what might seem like magic spun on fairy looms but is really as simple as a cotton shirt dried on a clothesline next to the honeysuckle vine before the sun is very high. It is the wading pool filled with cold water fresh from the hose, the discovery of an Earth-like planet deep in space, it is snail mail from a friend, something that was lost being found. We grow stable and centered through the appearance of miracles, through wonder, through joy. Float on, steady as she goes.

Wait

Patience, more a virtue than ever. The willingness to wait for whatever is desired but not yet here seems to appeal to very few. We wait for so much. Mostly I feel as though I wait for myself.

I wait for guidance, for information, for clarity. I've stopped hurrying. I allow matters to unfold in quiet and calm, if possible. If my inner wisdom is not a shrieking, "DO IT NOW," I will do it later. There was an article this week—somewhere—about procrastination not being only the refuge of slackers and layabouts. The article suggested there was wisdom at work when decisions were postponed, immediate action deferred.

(From the album, *The 2,000 Year Old Man* by Carl Reiner and Mel Brooks):

> *Carl:*
> *Sir, could you give us the secret of your longevity?*
>
> *Mel:*
> *Well, the major thing, the major thing is that I never, ever touch fried food. I don't eat it, I wouldn't look at it, and I don't touch it. And I never run for a bus. There'll always be another. Even if you're late for work, you know, I never run for a bus. I never ran. I just strolled, jaunty-jolly, walking to the bus stop.*

It seems the popularly-held belief is that we miss so much by delaying, delaying anything. I don't understand how this can be a universal truth. Since we have no way of knowing what even the next moment holds, how can we be certain that not taking the trip, not seeing the movie, not rushing out in pursuit of 12 seemingly essential activities will cause us lifelong regret. I have no "bucket list" and the name itself gives me hives. We can be led astray by our wants, just as we can be inspired by them.

I am not one of the universe's bold children, I never have been. Yes, I've done rash and foolish things, been incautious in dangerous ways. The luck of fools or an army of guardian angels. Haste is not my ally. Answers DO come, or if they don't I assume there is no answer. Rilke's urging that we live the questions is my norm. At times it seems to be only questions held loosely together by gravity. Wait, is what I interpret him saying. Wait.

Homesick

The homesickness of childhood, a harrowing first summer at camp or visit to the grandparents with distant relatives, even riding in their Cadillac, is of a different species than the homesicknesss of a more advanced age.

The longing for family and what is familiar, one's own bed and one's stuff, may give a context for the more existential version of the affliction as I have come to recognize it. I don't know if it is normal or pathological, the yearning for safe harbor, calm seas, reassurance and an external steadiness that life seldom offers.

Not a constant state, at least not a conscious one, this form of homesickness may be for something never experienced but dreamed of, idealized, sought. It may be for the return to an earlier time when, whether it actually was or not, existence seemed less fraught with uncertainty.

Jobs and paychecks are more illusion than reality. A roof of one's own is not a forever promise, nothing on the material plane is.

Home is a quiet mind. It is the willingness to lean into faith in the face of so few guarantees. It is acknowledging how much is unknown and uncontrollable and taking the next step anyway or standing still for a time, collecting my wits and other vulnerable parts. It is a refusal to be swept away by fear or despair, by all the answers I don't have.

We are pieceworkers, patching together security blankets out of what we can gather, out of what we know to be true and lasting—beauty, love without expectations, serenity and an extensive collection of files detailing everything that ever, against great odds, turned out well, evidence of good outcomes.

It is important for me to know and name this yearning. Otherwise, terror wins and I feel myself leaving *this* moment for tomorrow's shadowy corners. Yes, it is a rocket ride to someplace I've never been. It just might be home.

Elsewhere

With the exception of what tv meteorologists have come to call "monsoonal flow" here in Southern California and the general slime it creates on the skin, so far our summer hasn't been unbearable. Until the past several days. As I write this, our outside temperature is around 102. My wits left hours ago.

I learned about the Joffre Lakes a few days ago when my son's friend, a Vancouver resident for just a year, sent him her photos and description of the hike to reach them. I've never seen bodies of water that color. While I shiver in the winter when we are a mild 59 degrees, I no longer have any tolerance for heat. Our living room air conditioning unit, which I bless with all my heart, does its best. Southern California Edison calls me often with its "budget assistance alerts," telling me how far beyond my ideal bill I've surged. Images of elsewhere become refuge.

What a remarkable planet we inhabit. That a place as stunning as the Joffre Lakes isn't one of the seven wonders of the natural world speaks of our abundance. While pondering the list, I may take mental holidays to Victoria Falls, Mt. Everest, and the Great Barrier Reef. On days such as we've just experienced, my childhood wading pool would be every bit as enticing.

Part V

Amnesia

The words of the week could also be *tempus fugit* for the way in which time escapes from me or I wander off and fail to note its passing. An article found this week, *18 Ways Women Are Disconnected From Themselves*, by Falan Storm, brought the specifics of #18 in startling focus.

18. Limiting joy

> *Too many of us are not making time for the thing that most lights us up. Why does joy get put last? Because we are so disconnected with ourselves we don't realize the value, the importance and the sacredness of ourselves and how necessary joy truly is to our well-being.*

My best guess about this specific form of my amnesia is that it is habit-based, not something acute and current. It does have an aspect of putting more trivial things first, leaving no time or energy for what truly feeds the heart and spirit. When considered, it feels punishing. Visually, it comes with a stern, parental scowl and a no-dessert-til-you-eat-those-lima-beans admonition. All unspoken, of course.

What I don't do, or do too seldom or too little is, among other things, sing. Draw. Practice the ukulele. Write letters or at least notes using my dandy budget fountain pen. Create decorative envelopes to mail. If I understood this better, I could explain it, it would not be such a mystery. Because I do *feel* joy on a continuing basis, interspersed, of course, with flickering shadows cast by the past or the future, it doesn't seem like depression. What do I know?

I know I am not alone. This appears to be one of the ways our gender has been conditioned to behave. To consider, to honor, "the sacredness of ourselves" in ways great and small seems so easily postponed, deferred. I do not have a smart phone or tablet, yet can easily spend far too much time on my computer, on Facebook, on tracking down an artist or looking at pictures of pretty things. Even if I were 25 and not 70, time would be finite. Frittering it away, general farting about with the unimportant IS a dishonoring waste of all resources.

Perhaps we women can help each other escape these behaviors. You are welcome to ask me if I drew or sang today, or yesterday. Ask if I wrote to my aunt or cousin or any of my poet friends, the work of the hand and not the keyboard. I may try to dodge your questions if I am still practicing amnesia rather than art. I will ask you the same. How much genuine joy have you allowed yourself today? It is not about money or any material thing. It is only about love.

Cups, pots, bowls

To contain, hold, serve. Function and delight. In illustration, cups, bowls and pots are subjects that capture my attention. In life, in my kitchen, it is possible I could never have too many bowls, certainly never too many in melamine. Or green glass or yellow-glazed ceramic. A bowl is a happy thing.

Creatures

Our task must be to free ourselves by widening our circle of compassion to embrace all living creatures and the whole of nature and its beauty.

— Albert Einstein

As I wrote this over the weekend, I believe experts were still trying to find again, then free a blue whale who became tangled in fishing line off the coast of Los Angeles. To see the aerial footage of this 75-foot example of Earth's largest creature in our local waters is a remarkable experience, even from the comfort of the living room. The rescue team admitted they had no blue whale experience, they didn't know what the response might be to divers swimming close.

Hopping from nature to the world of art, I am enchanted by those who turn to the animal, insect, etc. kingdoms for inspiration. Last winter I found the work of felting artist Celestine and the Hare, her creatures and her humor which now brighten every day of my life. The list of illustrators who have charmed me over a lifetime would take days to compile. For now, I'll share the art of Wolf Erlbruch whose animals and others bring joy. Mister Finch creates arachnids and lepidoptera of unusual size to help populate our imaginations. Ceramic artist Midori Takaki has mastered the art of tapirs and softly-glazed polar bears.

I marvel at the ways in which the world can be both large and small simultaneously. The great blue whale and the statistic that perhaps only 5% of ocean life has even been identified, side by side with great silliness in a tiny package. Fall in love with as much as possible. It is all so miraculous.

Closure

Based on its standard usage, especially in tv news stories, I nominate *closure* for myth status. The states in which humans are left following death, illness, trauma and loss in its infinite forms do not lend themselves to tidy, invisible restoration. The frayed ends do not, in my experience, reweave themselves, things torn asunder do not simply reattach. What remains is not closure but a process of evolution, alchemy really, in which we move from being one thing to another. We find what ways we can to grow past the wound. It will never not leave a scar. That is not a mistake, that is order.

I believe well-intentioned, giving them the benefit of the doubt, people actually bully others into feeling they are doing it wrong, insisting that by some arbitrary time they should have reached "closure" with anything sad, often horrific. Unlike the previously mentioned news stories, I do not believe that a jury verdict, a death sentence, or an execution will ever bring to an end the sorrow and suffering resulting from criminal acts. A sense of revenge is not a substitute for diminished grief.

These musings spring from a post seen a few days ago, suggesting that if we can't have the illusive closure, we can learn to move on. To me, that is as good as it will get. Not to be mired in sadness at the same sharp level where we began is progress. Life alters us, in its high moments and its low. My familiar theme of living adaptively certainly applies to that which leaves us feeling broken and lost. Visualizing recovery from physical injury gives us a model of the multiple steps, the duration of healing to get us back on, for instance, our feet. And when therapy and exercises are completed, we may limp, we may not walk at all, yet we are not where we started.

To the best of my ability, I assume each of us is doing as well as we can, however imperfect that may appear. How can we possibly know what motivates another, what kind or insidious voices whisper suggestions that might even make sense in the moment? How can we know until it happens to us which events will take all the starch out of our spines and our spirits?

We will not, we cannot evolve until we learn to be much more forgiving with ourselves and our processes, until we come close to being kind to each other, no matter what. There will always be differences between us. We will always appear in the mirror as flawed, forgetting that flawed is human, the only material we have to work with.

I think my greatest disagreement with commonly held beliefs about closure is that it comes from somewhere outside of us, as with criminal proceedings where the jury awards closure to the victim's family. I think every bit of it is a deeply interior process. We are the almost unbearably slow train that brings us back to abandoned parts of ourselves. We must have patience beyond where we once thought patience ended. Everything is about becoming, to which there is no limit.

Steward

I feel it more and more, the insistence that I am, that each of us is, the steward of our own past. It begins to nudge me toward memoir, though not in a linear way. More likely fiction, however that may be achieved. Real stories, parts of which are true.

No matter how small we think our lives or our stories, they are pieces of an intricately entwined whole, pieces upon which other stories and lives balance or lean. We are not complete without each other.

As age drags us reluctantly or gleefully forward, that over which we are stewards expands. The more distant reaches do not shrink proportionately. Each minute, year, hour maintains its size. We simply let out our mental corsets to include new arrivals or, more accurately, to allow space for reinterpretation of all that has been. Events become clearer at a distance, we know ourselves better as we evolve.

The puzzle: how to weave the husbands, the missing but essential magazine issue, garage sale fashions, a backstage encounter, discovering martial arts movies, ghost towns, music, years of car trips, jewelry made of shells, hamburgers and ice cream, books and all the people into either a single strand or episodes of coherent narrative, even in my own mind let alone on paper.

We need not have survived the Titanic's sinking nor been Rosa Parks to have a story that deserves tending. Ordinary life is a series of wonders, our wonders, both unique and universal, begging our stewardship, whispering, Do Not Forget.

Listen

If you have become estranged from your intuition, all is not lost. The first step is to grow and remain quiet, still. The second is to listen. The third is to trust the information you receive no matter how unlikely, or even unreliable it seems. Knowledge greater than ours takes us in directions we would never have chosen.

The prompts are likely subtle. In my experience, intuition doesn't shriek. Notions of what to do next may arrive sounding similar to an overheard conversation, or may be the result of simply knowing something unknown a second before. Among my examples is the suggestion, several years ago as I began my morning at the computer, to "find more writers." Just that, not how, not where, not why. So I did. From that directive, I discovered poets, their blogs, their work, and ways my own writer's voice could become stronger, winnowing down the choice of words I needed for what I had to say. Those found writers became friends, models, teachers, even an angel who walked me through the poetry she'd studied her whole life. In one morning, based upon a flash of what I can only call intuition, my world expanded like a new universe being born.

Intuition, I believe, is the Panama Canal, moving us from one level of existence to another. We are lifted and transferred from ordinary to expanded. Intuition is not epiphany, not the explosive realization of discovery but something much softer, yet quietly insistent. It may lead us to epiphanies. to shouts of "eureka" and such. For me, its gifts, for they certainly are that, are neither noisy nor big, at least in the moment. In the aftermath of taking the recommended action, I may be aware that it was, in fact, a big deal. At which point, my normal response is to sit, subdued and at the same time dazed, grateful almost beyond measure. A sacred gift, indeed. Thank you.

Intuition is really a sudden immersion of the soul into the universal current of life, where the histories of all people are connected, and we are able to know everything, because it's all written there.

— Paulo Coelho (*The Alchemist*)

The high road

Among the things I have come to know or believe, one is that the high road is never a wrong choice. Any harsh words I can manage not to speak, any uncharitable thought I can dilute, any action I can take that leans more toward kindness gives me hope for myself and for all of us. The high road comes with strong visual support. I can see the forked path, one descending into shadow, miasma and murk, the other rising to fresh air (albeit possibly thin air) and sunshine. If we are gullible in our kindness, what is the harm? I know I will survive being a fool. It is not my job to figure out the motives of others as an excuse to behave ungenerously. Add this to the list of daily practices that I endeavor to include. Luckily, what we seek is progress, not perfection.

Goods

Goods and Services, Dry Goods, Fred C. Dobbs in *The Treasure of the Sierra Madre* referring to his rather meager possessions as his goods. Our stuff. Tools of our trade, our passion, our obsession. I am not, or not yet, one of the virtuous de-clutterers. I militantly defend my right to as many books, pens, blank envelopes and paper *goods* as I can afford (important) and accommodate. Need I even mention just how many things one can do with a piece of paper?

By my definition, goods differ from collections in their usefulness. We may never engage on a day-to-day basis with what we collect —or we may—but goods have a purpose. That purpose is to be used, even used up, though that is difficult when something is no longer made, can no longer be found. Discontinuances catch us by surprise. Such wailing, my own voice in my ears, when, without warning, Dennison stopped manufacturing those little slide-out cardboard boxes of red-bordered mailing labels or lick-and-stick gold notarial seals, for example. It seemed Trader Joe's Chili/Mango popsicles existed for two shopping trips before vanishing like the woolly mammoth. Fabric designs, scrapbook papers and sets of clear/cling rubber stamps have life spans like a mayfly. Blink and you've missed them. Try and track them down. Just try.

I often think of those brave, sturdy and determined types who settled the American West. I picture the trail, wagon following wagon in fair weather and misery. I see the goods that were too bulky, too heavy and of too limited a purpose being left behind. A harpsichord is generally what I imagine. Treasured, valuable, almost impossible to replace in the new life, but it will not feed them or keep them warm, no matter how it nourishes their souls. I would have made a very poor pioneer.

Mystery

Discussing possibly the best mystery ever, Josephine Tey's *The Daughter of Time*—a friend of my son's had just read it and was urging him to do so—brought to mind other classics, favorites, of the genre. To lounge about and read mysteries has been among life's great joys since I was in grade school.

Over many decades I've read my way through Dorothy L. Sayers, Rex Stout, Raymond Chandler, P.D. James, Dashiell Hammett, Carolyn Keene, Francis and Richard Lockridge, Josephine Tey, Elmore Leonard, Deborah Crombie. I've spent time with knitting mysteries, coffee house mysteries, scrapbooking mysteries, cat and/or dog mysteries, cooking mysteries, horse racing mysteries. I don't want to know, nor do I try to figure out who is responsible. Those are surprises I enjoy. Being the smartest guy in the room is seldom my goal.

I find life itself to be a daily mystery. It may intrigue or merely baffle. We have no idea how it comes out, other than that it does eventually cease. Every moment is a new unknown. There is much we can learn from the fictional sleuths for, in our way, each of us is a detective, following thin leads or playing our hunches. Intuition is a great ally, for many people will tell us any old thing. Knowing true from false is a desirable skill, one that can save us from some terribly unpleasant and startling moments. But it comes with the territory. At least everyday situations rarely leave us knocked unconscious, drugged with chloroform or attempting Houdini-like escapes. Simply keeping our wits about us and our spirits buoyant is enough of a task.

Being of the old school, still having a land line without caller I.D., brings its own unexpected encounters. Depending on the time of day, I may ignore any calls, see if there is a message or if it was just another robot. In Los Angeles, I suppose our biggest current mystery is whether or not it IS an El Nino year, whether it will rain and, if so, when and for how long and then what do we do? Venomous water snakes washing up on California beaches does not speak of good days to come.

The answer to most things is that we don't know. Like members of a book club all making their way through the same story, we keep turning the pages to see what's next. I promise to share any clue I find and hope you'll do the same.

Self-help

Let's say that we are in life as we may be in dreams, multiple characters in our own story. Victim and rescuer, speaker and listener, question and answer. This may sound like old business to many of you but it seems a fresh notion to me, brought on by my listening again to Beth Orton sing *Sisters of Mercy*. That may be us, "sisters of mercy," binding up our wounds.

As I participate in a meditation course on beliefs, the process carves open pockets of emptiness, even if just for a moment or two, space in which no debris has collected, places of possibility. Since I often feel what passes for real life is a bill of goods in which we are constantly being urged to reinvest, it is not such a leap for me to consider that much of what we've been told is essentially untrue, that it has always been untrue. Consider this: what if we are not the lesser beings we always felt ourselves to be.

So I walk around the edges of the song, the entire notion of mercy and deliverance, and wonder is it wholly interior work. If this is the true and natural order, our acting as self-healers, no wonder so many of us have grown quite elderly and weary waiting for rescue to come from external sources. As I say, this may be a familiar idea for you. I stopped looking at so-called self-help books decades ago, deciding it might be less exhausting to blunder along in a state of disrepair than to try and mend, according to one specific set of instructions or another, all that I believed was broken. In my long-ago experience with self-help, I never had the sense of it being a process which one undertook for the long haul, the gradual merging of this into that organically. The books or PBS presentations always seemed to half-promise remarkable and rapid transformation, desirable as we judged our present manifestation to be so unpalatable, so wrong.

For this same reason I don't read books in which women especially embark on a journey—physical/spiritual—of rather short duration after which they become, quite simply, THE light. Such journeys, the expense of them alone, and such starry outcomes are not within ordinary grasp. Few humans transcend in this fashion. We are not less if we illuminate a smaller patch. Again I return to an acknowledgement of process, of time and effort. That progress as we measure it may not be swift does not make it any less remarkable. At 70 years and counting, I will likely never believe there is a destination we reach in this lifetime.

We lay our own hands upon our hearts and souls. In our heads we repeat mantras that pull us closer to center. A quiet mind is the best friend I can hope for. As it seems to be the most workable choice, is it not okay to remain part caterpillar, part butterfly, 100% work in progress? It is the only solution I can imagine that moves us forward without discarding the best-loved and loyal parts of us, a bit threadbare though some may be, that have brought us this far.

Christmas magazines

Once upon a time I had a well-traveled, frequently-moved stash of December issues of all the house lovely magazines of the day. Decorations, recipes, wrapping, homemade gifts. Revisiting them each year was a source of inspiration and comfort. I'd collected them since the end of the 1960s, through the '70s and into '80s. Each year around this time, I'd pull out the stack and wander through them, one by one.

As I write this on Saturday, November 14, I recall how life's harder moments were softened by the sight of Christmas lights, thoughts of package wrapping to come, extravagantly decorated cookies that reminded me of those my mother created when my brother, sister and I were young children. It was the early 1950s and, until Martha Stewart introduced us to the art, perhaps in this century, I'd never seen anyone but our mom paint frosting on cookies. A woman ahead of her time.

Too many changes of residence, not really so many in the larger picture but enough that shifting *stuff* from place to place lost its luster. and one November day I realized that my mood-lifting magazines weren't with me. Earlier this year, an artist friend wrote to tell me she'd found on eBay a copy of the now-fabled and rare *House and Garden* December 1969 issue with the Gloria Vanderbilt Christmas and how it was all that she remembered before her copy had gone missing. Trust me when I tell you these are photos we would all look at through magnifying glasses, wanting to capture each shy figure or nuanced grouping. I was delighted for her and I wish there had been two copies.

I enjoy Christmas most by looking backward, at my own celebrations and those of others. I still harbor dreams of stumbling into the shuttered shop or flea market booth where all manner of extinct gift wrap nestles in dusty cellophane, for sale at its original price. When our hearts ache for any reason, we know instantly what will ease that sadness. Mary Engelbreit and Martha Stewart, with their ribbons and color are perfect companions for me today, offering a place on their pages where all is merry and bright. No more news, maybe fewer tears. I do not believe it is shallow to find solace in beauty and memories of joy. I believe those things exist exactly for that purpose.

Versatile

No matter how small the acreage of our fiefdom, we are required to be, among other things, the chief financial officer, social director, tech guy, scheduling secretary, chef, animal wrangler, medical intuitive, boundary-setting parent, and guru. And that is if we are only answerable to and responsible for ourselves. Increase the population and the list of jobs we must fill balloons to the size of a lesser moon. We tend to forget that we do, in fact, do it all.

On newspapers in the old days a reporter who took his or her own photos was called a combo man, a title I can claim for the occasional feature I sought out on a whim, no time to schedule a photographer. Nothing quite like a bright Saturday morning, a classified ads list of garage sales and my husband's Pentax on its rainbow strap around my neck. We have all worn many hats.

What necessary life positions do you fill on a daily or less frequent basis? What is required of you, or do you require of yourself, to keep the wheels turning? Imagine the length of our CVs as we might apply to be the captains of our own fates, if we did not already claim those titles.

Lost

Henry David Thoreau said, *"Not until we are lost do we begin to understand ourselves."* For today, perhaps many days, that is part of my story. Disquieting news arrived from more than one direction and, even though I feel I've found my way through part of it, bits of me have wandered off.

When lost, panic is pointless. What serves us is a version of treading water, staying in place, yet not idle. And companions, as they might be called, such as flat tin boxes of watercolors or *polychromos* (is it not a graceful word?) pencils. As I became lost while going about my life in my own home, I, in the only true preparedness I can claim, had emergency supplies on hand, including, in no particular order: a blank envelope, a pencil, a very fine-line waterproof pen, scissors, a glue stick, a sheet of white card stock, a Prismacolor Sunburst Yellow pencil, something red, glitter, color photocopies, paper for drawing, a good eraser, a rainbow ink pad, alphabet stamps. Bottled water and dark chocolate are also recommended to keep one company for the duration.

If there is a trick to what Thoreau described, it is to be lost long enough for awareness to sidle over and sit down, let us get caught up in its story and realize that lost is not who we thought it to be.

In dreams

As I've mentioned before, I don't feel that making other people hear about our dreams would qualify as good manners. Therefore I won't tax you with the dream narrative, other than to say a friend took a group of us to a hodgepodge of a book store and before any of us could leave we each had to buy at least one pair of red shoes.

Even if only in theory, no longer so much in practical life, I have an abiding love for red shoes. In a happiness hierarchy for manufactured objects, they might top the list.

I can only guess at the workings of the mind when suddenly overloaded with information impossible to digest, to process. What I can say is that the past week brought (as of this writing) two nights of dream movies that warmed and gladdened me, that restored balance when we'd all been tipped overboard, that gave me what felt like real time spent with a friend I see too seldom. In addition, I was offered the delight of red shoes, tucked under counters all over the dream shop, the Easter egg hunt-style search for the right pair or two, an enormous squash that held pages to a mysterious manuscript and the fact that I was, as I always am in my dreams, younger, stronger and much more able-bodied.

What I assume is this, based on no scientific evidence at all: rather than shut down in a state of no-thought, my mind, and possibly yours, took me by the hand on a Lewis Carroll adventure to places where the nonsensical made sense. It took me to spend time with favorite people and things, safe places, sunny or happy or curious places for which I was absolutely present. If there is some overarching order to our lives, my sleeping mind drove the getaway car that rescued me from the latest unthinkable events and delivered me to a version of home, home for the heart where I wasn't teetering but steady, from which I could step into the day not fearful but comforted. Wearing new red shoes.

Hidden recesses

Waters for which there are no charts, roads without signposts, sealed rooms, locked chests, diaries written in invisible ink, we are much bigger inside than we appear. We are stewards of realms real and imagined, explorers for the ages, inventors, students. What I know to be true for me is that I make it up as I go along. How could I do it otherwise when each moment brings new possibilities? I gobble up information, ideas, images and offer them a home within. We are capacious creatures, our castles of self containing too many rooms to count. For whatever knowledge we seek or skill we wish to master, there is space. We cannot outgrow a curious mind, a questing spirit.

Luminous

Aglow with an inner light, achieved in paintings with great skill. Achievable in life by finding a brave and gentle and loving path through whatever a day holds. A lifetime's work and no easy task.

In a recent dream, most of which is forgotten, a long-time friend referred to me as luminous. I could think of no compliment I would treasure more. Aspirations of luminosity.

To be the beam that reaches darkest corners, to be a source of warmth for any spirit too long in the cold, to illuminate, to brighten, to carry or be the lantern so that others aren't left behind, that is what Anatoly Timoshkin's angel paintings suggest. Serenity, contemplation, knowing. This week brings the year's longest night, when we all might wish winter on its way. It brings memories of childhood Christmases when, as now, the lights were what I loved most.

May we continue to fan the flames in each other and ourselves, keep the fires lit against all that would have us fearful and lost. Especially together we are so much greater than the dark.

Things we are not

Our size or shape. Our infirmities. Our diagnoses. Our age.

Our income or material possessions.

Our pasts, our wounds, our disappointments.

Our previous unwise choices.

Among the usual suspects.

One-hit wonders.

Over the hill.

Things we are

Your past is just a story
And once you realize this
It has no power over you.

— Chuck Palahniuk

Made of star stuff.

There are days when I honestly feel that the size of my feet may be a crime against humanity. Same for the way I seem to order (?) my life by piles, my tendency to procrastinate, the slow speed at which I move.

I am not, you are not any of those things, regardless of the fact that they do exist. That is all they do, exist. They are not us.

There is a tendency among most humans to view our flaws (by our definition) as being, at best, only slightly less horrendous than a rip in the space/time continuum. We are fully capable of punishing ourselves for varying from an ideal. The parts of us that show carry most of the blame. Likely we have been struggling under those burdens for a lifetime.

What we are is capable of learning to love, with mad passion and without reservation, ourselves. It is no longer acceptable, not that it ever was but that didn't stop us, to go picking about with tweezers and dental probes among the moments and incarnations of our pasts to find the hurtful, humiliating, couldn't-you-just-die parts and feasting on them.

They happened, they are not us, we are not them. Exposed to time and the elements, even granite turns to dust.

No matter what there has been, each morning delivers a new day. Each of those days carries us further from the past. It is so much harder to shine when we labor under our own imagined shadows.

Softer

This will, no doubt, be the year of many things, not the least of which for me is The Year of Growing Softer. We are not meant to be our carapaces, spiny ridges, jagged corners. We are not intended to live defended lives, though it may feel otherwise. Without growing softer, how do we begin to flow into each other, how do we empathize?

Growing softer is, like much of life, a process. It is not achieved in one herculean leap. If it is realized at all, it will be through tiny, elfin steps, wearing Barbie's pumps on our fingertips and walking with all the style we can muster through minefields, real and imagined. "They" are an illusion. There is really only "Us."

Clay

My mother was a ceramic artist. She began with clay and the last works she created were made of clay. In between she was known for her paintings and collages. When, in later life, she produced a line of ceramic "kids" as she called them, they helped her travel to dreamed-of destinations like the Greek islands and to Spain to see Gaudi's architecture first-hand.

More and more, whatever wisdom guides me tells me that I have all I really need to make life, myself and my art into what I want. The absence of some material object is not what stands between me and the far shores of my mind. There are ways, there are always ways. That we cannot see or name them today is no indication that they don't exist. I have never believed that we are here on earth to be tried, tested. This is not trial by ordeal in spite of the moments it feels precisely like that.

I find that simple works better for me than complicated, plain seems a better match than fancy. What spoke to me through Elizabeth Price's ceramic women was an unmistakable sense of the extraordinary to be found in the ordinary. In form, I see her gently glazed figures as straightforward, involved in the task at which we find them. Yet my sense is of the years of living which brought them to these moments. Cumulative. We are cumulative creatures, products of time and experience, thoughts and actions, being and doing and puzzling over the meaning of it all.

Perhaps it all just is. We just are, nothing more impenetrable than that. A day of one foot in front of the other, in fair weather and foul. Strength and courage for what comes, patience, infinite patience with ourselves and others. A ceramic woman who holds the chicken, do we need to be told the story or can we draw a conclusion from the fact of them? Price's woman in the yellow hat, any one of us in a pointed yellow hat. I'm guessing her feet are bare as the feet of Price sculptures usually are. All their gazes are focused on what we cannot see.

What I forget some mornings, as I *think* myself into the day, is that being, most likely, is my greatest challenge and clearest calling. To be, as clay, still and present, container of trouble and joy, of hope and doubt, alternately certain and mystified. To navigate without fuss and drama the unblazed path of today. To leave the big Ta-Dos in the hands of those for whom they are better suited. As we are told of Stuart Little,

> *He wiped his face with his handkerchief, for he was quite warm from the exertion of being Chairman of the World. It had taken more running and leaping and sliding than he had imagined.*
>
> — E. B. White, *Stuart Little*

Origami

Reasons why I began poking around origami envelope how-tos this week:

Something for my brain and hands to do together.

Valentine potential.

Paper obsession.

Envelope ditto.

The idea took hold when I saw Rachel Hazell's step-by-step from a series of guest blogs she did for *Flow* magazine on a love letters workshop she taught last fall in Paris. A Google search will lead you to the Heart Envelope Project.

Paper folding, especially in the beginning stages, is a focused and peaceful activity. It requires full presence. I've realized over the years that I remember a craft lesson better when I have experienced it hands-on. And when I've repeated and repeated and repeated it. We all have our styles of learning and mine is most efficient when I let my hands talk to my brain.

Crafting with paper has been a joy since girlhood. My hands, at times, are a bit less steady, less predictable than they once were. Origami seems a task at which they still function consistently and as expected. I leave the worktable feeling reasonably masterful. Anything that matters takes time, it also takes practice. Origami offers the opportunity to develop skills. I defer to *Napoleon Dynamite* on "skills":

Pedro: Do you think people will vote for me?
Napoleon Dynamite: Heck yes! I'd vote for you.

Pedro: Like what are my skills?

Napoleon Dynamite: Well, you have a sweet bike. And you're really good at hooking up with chicks. Plus you're like the only guy at school who has a moustache.

Tend

To apply one's self to the care of. To watch over.

How do we see to one another, not allow any of us to disappear beneath the waves of ordinary misfortune? That, I believe, is our Work.

My list of Those Most Dear leans toward the simultaneously blessed and cursed whose minds and works reveal them to be angels, possibly gods in human form to whom sorrow is no stranger.

Poets, musicians, writers, painters, performers, shamans, Samaritans, cooks, teachers, healers, fliers at all altitudes, entrepreneurs, intuitives, we are all richer for what you bring to our days. That your own days have been, and frequently continue to be filled with illness, loss, trauma, lack, terror, pain and bewilderment has not stopped you, has rarely slowed you down.

My tending, if such were possible, would be a continual disbursement of care packages filled with everything you need most: health, peace, strength, optimism, guarantee of a desired outcome, the meeting of every possible physical, material and spiritual need, humor and music and beauty and light and love. My tending would bring, to the outer edge of anyone's ability, safety. The unknown will always be part of this existence but it would not be the lurking, crouching thing-behind-the-door that it has become. A margin of security is not too much to ask.

I would walk you in your fishbowl, groom and stroke your dear warty head, smooth your collar and see that your necktie was properly knotted. I would send what is warm (or cool) and bright, lend my own solid arm to lean upon, install elevators where needed and employ reliable, skilled craftspeople to fix whatever required mending. Going without would no longer be the only option.

My life is continually blessed and illuminated by those who tend to me. One profound reminder of such tending hangs on my bedroom wall, an assemblage that proclaims, "I get by with a little help from my friends." So do we all.

Small magic

I believe in magic. Whether sleight of hand or sleight of mind, I believe we perform it. It is part of the current that carries us through. Unsung, perhaps never mentioned, the multiple acts of small magic with which we conjure on a daily, or more frequent basis serve to levitate us above, well, all that isn't magic.

No need to pretend that life does not deliver leaden moments, sleepless nights, hand-wringing and tears of oh-so-many descriptions. It is small magic that rescues us from being wedged into those tight spots we thought inescapable.

My magic list includes (as I've mentioned so often) the color red, being surprised at my own explosive laughter, friends and family and love, each new day, sleep, encouraging words, good news, our Southern California version of stormy weather, really delicious coffee, getting warm when I'm cold, signs of intelligent life, the fact that people play music and write books and make movies, the experience of impossible things happening, all wonders created by man and nature, the ability to change my mind, dark chocolate (alas, in moderation), poetry (in unlimited quantities), kindness, beauty, making things with my hands.

There is no true magic too small to be counted. The simple act of noticing, of knowing, makes us participants. "Is THIS your card?" Astonishment, admiration. "Yes, that's my card." How many moments in a day deliver impossible results no less remarkable.

And this, the power of words, the minds and souls to which we turn for incantations:

She conceived of life as a road down which one traveled, an easy enough road through a broad country, and that one's destination was there from the very beginning, a measured distance away, standing in the ordinary light like some plain house where one went in and was greeted by respectable people and was shown to a room where everything one had ever lost or put aside was gathered together, waiting.

— Marylinne Robinson, *Housekeeping*

In spite of

Let us go forth, the tellers of tales, and seize whatever prey
the heart longs for, and have no fear. Everything exists,
everything is true, and the earth is only a little dust under our feet.

— W.B. Yeats

I experience periods of time during which I don't know much of anything. Trying to keep one's mind a clear path seems an almost laughable goal. Yet without the continual removal of debris with which we are bombarded, stuck becomes the only option.

So. For the sake of peace and what might pass for sanity, I ignore the news as much as possible. I refuse to engage in debate and carping. I try not to develop spontaneous headaches over the nitpicky nettles of life such as outsourced tech support or customer service. As best I can, I soldier on in spite of matters concerning health, finances and the frequently challenging business of living adaptively as an elderly creature, for there are always two sides to the ledger.

Kristin Vestgard's paintings show women as luminous beings in mist-filled surroundings that soften the harder edges of existence. Harsh noises are muffled by fog, even the warning horn brings comfort. It speaks of safe harbor, of being watched over.

Growing up during the days of air raid drills, images of atomic apocalypse always fresh, probably gave birth to the in-spite-of state of mind. Just as I've decided not to worry about other cosmic bodies colliding with Earth or our Milky Way galaxy (Andromeda edges closer, but 4 billion years is by any measure a long time), I have the choice to surrender to reasonable fear over all that is unknown or to try and reach beyond that reality and catch hold of something different.

It seems I am responsible for the balance of my mind and the quiet of my spirit. The in-spite-of option is not the same as being an ostrich. I do know what's going on out there. I don't choose to let it overtake what I also know to be true. Like the once-popular song about walking on the sunny side of the street, "I used to walk in the shade with the blues on parade." I'm still in the process of recovering from most of a lifetime of angst, a process almost as slow as the predicted Milky Way/Andromeda collision. I write of this for a recent morning brought unquiet moments when I stepped away from my preferred *modus operandi.* I felt the disturbance in every part of my body.

My antique dealer brother-in-law tells of an auctioneer he knew early on in his collecting career, a man who would offer an item for bid and describe it as being " . . . broke, but it ain't broke bad." Ain't broke bad may be just good enough.

Vamping

Of course we make it up as we go along. There is no clear path. Of course we are frequently left to improvise, tread water and vamp, "repeat a short, simple passage of music," until rescue arrives or we grow weary and abandon the project.

What we forget when life is lurching along in a mostly familiar way is that we are generally vamping, too, for very little occurs on our schedule in the manner we would prefer. When we are thoroughly becalmed, kept from our tasks and purpose, the business of making it up becomes an even more essential skill. I miss my daily computer time, I miss my friends and the words we share, I miss the images of beauty which nourish me. And I know this is likely a shallow response, a First World problem, yet in a quiet, not especially mobile and rather sequestered existence, I do feel it as a loss.

On the plus side, I had ample time to create mail art for an exchange (front AND back). I've been rereading *Housekeeping* by Marilynne Robinson, in spite of finding it so much more bittersweet all these years later. A quantity of experiences, once known, can be sobering. I have not swept an afternoon nap into the corner in favor of just another hour, give or take, at the keyboard, only to feel rest's absence as the evening wears on. I have even more time to commune with the combination of nothing and my silence.

"Take nothing for granted" is always giving me the knowing wink and pointy elbow. "Count your blessings" is moment-by-moment thought. Right now I'm not sure if the computer or its unavailability is the blessing.

Glimmer

Just a bit of sparkle, a beam of hope that it has not all gone south. It can take the simplest form: old prescriptions that now require no co-pay, happy mail art, mild days and a kickass basketball game. Spirits can flag as Life goes about the business of being Life, as friends experience enormous loss, bewildering illness, setbacks. It is easy to lose what felt like solid footing. We sense an overload of stress-induced chemicals. Some of us—no names, please—get the shakes.

Yet restoration, that essential glimmer of better times, either at hand or to come, is not beyond our grasp. A nap with real, deep and even dreaming sleep can transform me. On some days my Pollyanna-esque M.O. has frayed, lost some of its dependable starch and it takes greater effort to find my way back. My fall-back affirmation continues to be, "I'm still here."

Dr. Hunter S. Thompson has been credited, and I have no call to doubt it, with the sentiment, "When the going gets weird, the weird turn pro." To which I say, "If only." I am so ready for a paying gig that matches my uncommon skills.

Options

For the sake of this post and not as an absolute, let us assume that things happen for reasons, usually known in hindsight. If ever.

As I rely on my son's tutelage and his iPad—and one-fingered typing—until we are computer compliant again, I have returned to reading. Somehow that lifelong pleasure was shuttled aside as I found how few activities could actually fit into a day. My delighted book companions may be heard cheering, "We're BACK!"

I began with the rereading of Marilynne Robinson's *Housekeeping*, which I found so much more bittersweet these several decades later (forgive me if I already wrote of this). Almost too many experiences of loss now stuffed into my bag of tricks, I inhabit the story in a different skin.

Then Junot Diaz's *The Brief Wondrous Life of Oscar Wao*, winner of the Pulitzer and a lesson in history of the Dominican Republic as well as life, in all caps, in buzzing neon, as one family lives it. I cried at the ends of these first choices.

Now, a decision: the somehow-missed Cormac McCarthy *Blood Meridian*, Ursula Le Guin's *Left Hand of Darkness* or my birthday gift of *Jonathan Strange and Mr. Norell*, the mini-series version of which I truly loved.

I am not confused, imagining that my brief and current reading list is any sort of stop-the-presses news. Simply, I choose to share the yet-again discovered truth that all which seems at first so impossibly vexing may actually be not all bad. Among my manifesto-level beliefs is that complaining and/or whining is a poor use of time, a poorer use of finite energy. Let us find, always, the brightest sides we can and pledge them our allegiance. Any other option is pure suckage.

Let's dance

The puzzle, or one of them: how to replicate the joy, the freedom, the sense of pure abandon one finds through dance when one's legs no longer agree to participate.

The adaptive life. Life, indeed, no mistaking it, though of need being more inventive: when the roads are washed out, how do we reach our destination?

I have not yet thrown myself fully into all possible avenues of movement available to one of less than full mobility. I have an excellent book on chair yoga, mostly unexplored, and the wits to know one can do a lot of shoogling about without standing, certainly without what could be identified as walking. Yet I delay, or perhaps resist is not too strong a word. What is it in the human psyche that allows and even goads us to hold ourselves back from that which could be so freeing? Or should I say, in MY psyche. I have no clear answer.

If life is about adapting, and it is, even for the most able-bodied, it is also about resisting our natural default positions. On an intellectual level I know the more I move, the more accomplished I feel; the more I move, the more alive and youthful and hopeful I feel. Many, many years ago I was a ballet student. My body remembers how that felt. I know what my legs were able to do. What is the purpose of imagination if not to elevate us beyond actual or perceived limitations?

As this serves, I hope, as pep-inducing self-talk, it may throw needed illumination into our collective shadowed corners. Our time here is finite, of which I am too aware on a regular basis. That there is ample peace and delight in my days is not enough, not when I am capable of creating more through simple acts. My history contains loss and trauma, as, I'm sure, yours does, too.

For so many of us there has already been too much juiciness lost to sorrow. Let's swear to keep reminding each other. It will never be too late to dance.

Contain

As I look at the packet of de-stashed envelopes, bought for a song on Etsy, sliding from shades of banana cream pie yellow, through sherbet hues to those of a spring garden, I think about Easter baskets, for the colors shriek spring. I think about long-ago kits for dying eggs and the smell of vinegar. I think about new lace-edged ankle socks for church. I think about other times.

How is it possible for us to contain all we have known and encountered on this voyage? What a miracle that we manage to sift and sort and store it for, we hope, retrieval as needed. The wonder of the body remembering how it felt to crouch and bend while hunting the hidden eggs, the nests of jelly beans, the growing weight of the basket with each added find. Do we imagine the memory because we know it happened or are we there once again?

I am a fan of boxes, bags, cabinets and drawers, places and means for the storage of goods. To have and to hold and to carry. I admire friends who have committed written works to memory, something for which I once had a talent. The array of material, of subjects, for which our minds and bodies are repositories is without limit. Every skill we've acquired, from a foreign language to knitting, remains stashed in some infrequently visited corner, possibly a diluted version of what it once was, but there even if as a more ghostly presence.

We are encyclopedic in ways we may not recognize. Recipes, meals pleasurable or otherwise, conversations, places, scents, clothes that fit or didn't, a sibling's smile, fear or anticipation, every emotion, every sense, ideas, awarenesses, they fill us yet leave room for more. To be is to contain. Here's to spring and our capacity for the infinite.

Plan B

In things both great and small, one finds reprieve and deliverance by having made, in advance, a second choice. That it was second does not proclaim it lesser. Often it turns out to be the preferred option, which is only known when Plan A falls through or vanishes like the mirage it may have always been. In my experience, the potential for self-delusion is without limit.

Plans B (or Plan Bs) demand invention, improvisation. They allow us to act out our frequently under-employed talents as magicians, those clever sorts who can save a fallen souffle or fashion the missing element of an incomplete Halloween costume, moments before the curtain rises. A classic Plan B invariably requires the replacement or circumvention of a missing essential. Dropped the keys to the getaway car? Plan B. Broken zipper, power outage, balky printer, insufficient funds, etc., Plan B. Priority Mail (flat rate) is a procrastinator's ideal fall-back. The panache to pull off eccentric choices in hair or make-up or clothing can disguise Plan B fixes.

So many of our expectations turn out to be unrealistic fantasies, leaving two choices: withering with disappointment for an extended period, like forever, or acknowledging that we are stuck with IT, whatever IT is, and would be wise to go back into the huddle and come up with an alternative play. The truth is that life frequently has plans that bear no resemblance to ours, though they may turn out to be ultimately preferable.

I don't recall seeing the word "flexibility" on a list of classic virtues, though it belongs there with patience, generosity and courage, as a means to overcome adversity and lack. For us, masters of Plan B, there is a sufficiency, regardless of how it first appears.

Part VI

Be here now

I may let Ram Dass, author of *Be Here Now*, speak for himself through some best-known quotes. You will find them on Goodreads.

For myself, awake on Sunday morning after an insufficient sleep, my first thought was to speak of it—complain, as it were—as though that would be a proper substitute for being awake too much of the night. There were two choices: be here, in this moment, groggy yet sun-touched and present, or be there, in the grip of insomnia brought on by who-knows-what, fretting, wondering if I'd get to sleep before the night was gone. I chose Door #1.

Solid ground only exists for me in this moment. If I wander into the past as anything other than an interested visitor, I invariably manage to feel shame, remorse, guilt and sorrow for the choices I did or did not make. Time has allowed me to become kinder to my past self but there are scenes glimpsed in the rear-view mirror that still give me the whim-whams. The future is so unknowable that travel there is the definition of folly. I hope, I guess, I try to will the outcome I think may put everything right, guarantee all that cannot possibly be promised. Or I dread, I fear, I worry. What a goose.

The art of being here, and only here, now is one I practice constantly, as an apprentice in any field would. In my favor is the fact that I now know the different options offered by present, past and future, know that two of them are chump choices. Mindfulness, a word for another week, helps keep me out of the swampiest places.

Life

It was a weekend of treats, two movies with no explosions, interstellar travel, explicit language or ass kicking. Not that I have anything against such pictures. Far from it. However, there are times when storytelling in a lower key is a better match.

On my sister's recommendation, we saw *Brooklyn*, which allowed the two of us to bring out our favorite moments for discussion and agreement. Such details as the department store's pneumatic tube system recalled our childhoods. The sweet and gentle exploration of life as some have lived it gave a needed respite from wearying, real-world harshness. We took to heart various aspects of the immigrant experience, very much a part of almost all our histories, certainly my sister's and mine. And I happily confess to being a fool for Irish music.

Look for the trailer for a Chinese film, *A Simple Life*, another quiet segment of the human experience, dealing with love and respect, growing old and, by my definition, managing, as best one can, to adjust to life's demands.

It seems to me that there are as many ways to be part of the human family as there are humans. Every story ever told explores the infinite variations, unique responses, choices made. The best stories remind me that no one, no one, has it easy. How a thing appears from the outside is no true measure. Hooray for the movie-makers, all those names scrolling past once the picture ends. Hooray and thank you. My world continues to expand.

Prevail

Were it possible to reveal a cross-section of life, I know we would appear just as rings of the giant redwoods, as geological strata depicting ages of ice, of flood, of fire.

In spite of so much, many of us, perhaps most, prevail, transcending circumstances. That we differ from the rocks, the redwoods, in remembering events that marked us may impair our ability to claim progress. I am sure such memories, along with the times of trauma, loss, abuse and general bewilderment they preserve, have obscured my clear view of what some might call a version of radiance, of success, for surviving is success.

It is easier to see triumph over grim epochs marked by terror in others than in myself. I could list for friends who have prevailed over impossible odds the treasures they somehow smuggled away from crippling pasts. That we traverse multiple incarnations in one lifetime I have no doubt. We can say that each event changes us or we can recognize those changes as essential layers upon which an authentic self is built. How could we have gotten here if we hadn't been there?

The number of years I spent attempting to put myself back together, to be repaired or restored to a norm that never existed, surely exhausted resources which could have been put to more enjoyable use. At the time the damage seemed so great, the need for fixing so urgent, and perhaps it was.

There are moments in which I know I've found my song, others in which it is hard not to see how I do life as falling short of my own expectations, let alone those of others. To be enough by the only standard that really matters, our own, requires compassion, patience and unconditional love of a staggering magnitude.

Not to be the glass half-empty—or more—as the result of circumstances so far beyond our control takes industrial-strength optimism and beyond that faith that there is invisible order in apparent chaos and distress. We prevail where and as we do, through what brings us joy, what showcases our sometimes bizarre and freakish strengths, what seems like rare good fortune shining upon us. In truth, this benevolence is not rare. It is consistent and real. We simply need to grow into it, give ourselves and it time to become what we'd been waiting for.

Epistle

As we round the final turn of April, National Letter Writing Month, as well as National Poetry Month, I realize that my epistolary intentions have, once again, not been matched in reality. I have nothing to offer in my defense, other than the feeble and familiar declaration that time evaporates. While I sleep or putter, it shrivels like a puddle under an August sun, leaving me here with plans for witty or heartfelt correspondence and a boatload of pens and paper.

I have sent some notes, a few parcels, a tag or two, even a brief letter written with a fountain pen, one of my higher aspirations. In case you have doubts on the subject, the fountain pen, in my opinion, is indication that civilization is not extinct. I am thankful the ink cartridge was invented though I am not finished with pens that still drink from exotically-labeled bottles. The color choices of fluid ink—and the names they carry—leave me and my kind more than a little woozy.

Reading this week's edition of *The Marginalian*, I learned that letters written between Marie Curie and the man she loved after Pierre's sudden death were stolen and published by a reptilian press to humiliate and discredit her. She was championed in those grim days by Albert Einstein, whom she had recently met at an invitational science conference. Einstein, of course, sent his encouraging words via letter.

Regrets deplete us, they stunt our dreams of forward momentum, yet I wish I had saved so many more of the letters I received over a lifetime. To see familiar handwriting, feel again the quickened pulse brought on by that hoped-for return address in the envelope's corner, would mean more than I could have imagined.

Letters mingle souls, so we've been told and so I believe. Before April vanishes in the mist, shall we vow to write at least one, or one more, meaningful epistle to one beloved soul? I know we will all be the better for it. Yours sincerely.

It will be okay

Hello, May.

Recently I heard a description of core values in three words: JOY, MINDFULNESS, and COMPASSION. That I can't remember the source goes with the territory. I do remember this much, that I agreed with them. Life has, and takes, every opportunity to turn our hearts hard, shrinking them to rock-like nuggets that resist chewing, chipping and melting. This is not the right answer.

For myself, my son and all of us for whom recent circumstances appeared, however briefly, to be heading south, don't believe it. How a thing looks or seems and what it actually is are galaxies apart. What do we know, really? Old fears, ancient beliefs, tell us their version of truth. In order to prevail, we must turn away from such defeating thoughts. Here is how I pictured it today: my mind is the hysterical quasi-friend whose hair is always on fire.

Take a moment for tears or terror, then, in the absence of an answer, let it go. My son has said to me so many times, "It will be okay. We'll be okay." And we're still here. It is not a hollow promise but a knowing. It is trust. Into the midst of these musings came a phone call, it has been a good season for those. The caller and I have history spanning some 46 years, or near to it. That often the simple sound of the other's voice makes us laugh reminds me, not that I had forgotten, what good medicine this is. Love is the vein of gold we strike when seeking our fortunes, here on this swiftly tilting planet. It continues to take me by surprise, which makes its worth that much greater. It may not all be exactly how or what we thought we wanted when we set out to conquer the world or at least grow a ribbon-worthy patch of giant pumpkins or towering hollyhocks, here by our feet. Regardless, it will be okay.

Minimum daily requirement

Eat an apple every day,
Get to bed by three,
Oh, take good care of yourself
You belong to me.

— from *Button Up Your Overcoat*
lyrics by B. G. (Buddy) DeSylva & Lew Brown,
music by Ray Henderson

It is part of my manifesto or perhaps mantra, color is a nutrient. As is beauty, however you define it. While certain resources may grow thin from time to time, we are kept steady and strong by that which feeds the spirit. Added, of course, to the daily apple and the likes of vitamin D. Sufficient sleep, laughter in excess, for there can never be too much, and ditto for kindness in all directions, make us mighty or at least above average. They help us cope, transcend the bumpy interludes, keep us in good fettle.

In *The House at Pooh Corner*, Kangaroo gave Roo and Tigger malt extract as "strengthening medicine." I have held that thought my entire life, coming to identify certain, let's call them nostrums, as my strengthening medicines. Last week in one of those internet articles on how to make your life better was the suggestion to send a thank you note every week. Simple, right? Good manners, the chance to create mail art, something we would all like to receive. My strong intention is to add it, with thanks for the idea. The more full our bag of shoring-up tricks, the less apt we are to sag or falter.

For today and every day, let us be generous with ourselves in thoughts and acts that sustain us. Life can feel like a daunting assignment if one is undernourished. Do what is necessary and please, take good care of yourself.

Mild

Mild, as in gentle, patient, soft-spoken. Unfrenzied. A state more rare than one might suppose. Try and be all of those simultaneously or even in succession. Yet mild seems the true low-key antidote to rage, outrage, umbrage, any knee-jerk response to what displeases us. Let it go. Choose your battles. Taking huge and noisy offense as a chronic state cannot be good for any organs. Even as a witness and not a participant, it causes me discomfort.

Balance may be one of the virtues. It indicates a sturdy steadiness, a skill which I picture being practiced just as any acrobatic art, over and over with numerous missteps. Arriving at mild by way of extreme seems the natural path. To be peaceful in the midst of escalating chaos may appear to indicate a state of being unclear on the concept. Why aren't you shouting? Because someone needs to find and hold the quiet center, someone needs to remember proportion, someone needs to be the water that silently and subversively wears down the rock.

Mild might be called an ideal, a desired but nearly unreachable state, an aspiration. My experiment will be this: to see how many times I don't lose my cool in the course of a day, a normal day of TV news, internet witlessness, ordinary things going wrong. Mild is not a synonym for uncaring, for anaesthetized, for MIA. At best it can help keep the roar quieted, the rhetoric more civilized. A one-sided argument is a bullying soliloquy. Imagine us being civilized with each other. A girl can dream.

Avian

We've been on earth all these years and we still don't know for certain why birds sing.

— Annie Dillard, *Pilgrim at Tinker Creek*

Our suburban neighborhood, crowded with street traffic because of a never-completed freeway connection, is becoming more and more an open-air aviary. This side street, with its power lines still strung overhead, is the site of regular shifts in the avian population, as though the bird chiefs got together to draw up a schedule, who perches where and sings when.

Friday morning, after years of occasional honking flyovers, we saw our first pair of geese, labeled birds for this discussion. Just after daybreak they took up position on a roof across the street and beat the green Amazon parrots to the task of waking the neighborhood. Throughout the night, a lone peacock on a nearby hill issues its nearly human-sounding cry, distant enough not to interrupt my sleep. A dedicated red-beanied woodpecker returns daily to a smooth-trunked palm tree for what we hope is gourmet fare in great abundance. His kin prefer the rough bark of a closer, shorter palm and tolerate being driven away occasionally by a crow's superior size and wingspan.

In warmer, less windy weather, hawks circle above vacant lots, parkland and the high school's playing fields. I am no longer close enough to hear their distinctive cries as I could when we lived just below the mountains. Mockingbirds, mourning doves, the familiar crows and parrots, a pigeon or two, regular hummingbirds and myriad unidentified songbirds may visit and/or serenade our block throughout the day. The parrots are often so raucous that we can't hear the television. The same can sometimes be said of law enforcement helicopters.

With time and the inclination for sky hypnosis, we have come to know when there's a new bird on the block. Without binoculars, I cannot consider myself a true bird watcher. I may not know why they sing, I just know how happy I am that they do.

Impossible

I never dreamed, or more accurately, I never thought ahead to where writing a blog might take me. It has brought me here, of all impossible things. Consistency over time, a subject which, were it a class in school, I believe I'd be failing. And not only consistency but the incomparable pleasure of it. I resist counting as best I can for I believe so much of value is unquantifiable. And yet.

Fairly early in my association with Rubbermoon Stamps, I drew a simple image that says:

IMPOSSIBLE
THINGS
HAPPEN

The stamp remains part of the collection and is more true, at least for me, than it was nearly 20 years ago when it debuted. I find there is room for impossibilities to take up residence when I stop doing limiting things. Fixed notions, fear, worry, narrow vision, pessimism, such thoughts must be surrendered before the impossible feels safe enough to remove its disguise and knock on the door.

Welcoming the impossible seems to be a matter of allowing, getting out of the way so it has room and time to work. It is a highly independent agent, resisting invitation while surpassing any secretly held expectations. Its greatest delight seems to be our astonishment. When it arrives, make note of the circumstances, write a sentence on the calendar, use an exclamation point, tell your friends, give thanks. Be a grateful and gracious recipient. It will likely visit again.

Tiny stitches, baby steps

As long as the world is turning and spinning,
we're gonna get dizzy
and we're gonna make mistakes.

— Mel Brooks, *The 2,000 Year Old Man*

Seeing samples of very small embroidery stitches by artists on Facebook, it seemed such a wise approach to a complex, lengthy task. Teensy. Wee. Such a sharp and slender needle, such a fine thread. We are held together without our stuffing starting to leak by delicate, intentional work of hand and eye and heart. I will, I swear, regardless of the years and decades I have done it otherwise, take whatever time it requires to steward meaningful aspects of myself and my wild, precious life. Even with excruciating caution, one gets dizzy and makes mistakes.

I no longer believe that quantity is the equal of quality. I have attended with unblinking focus the handwork of artists shown in documentaries about the great fashion houses. I am slow and can just, just, be present for one next indicated thing at a time, one bead, one stitch. When my mind begins to run away with—or from—me, I reel it back in and take up where I was before becoming lost. Regardless of what many try to sell us, this is not a contest, not with others and not with ourselves. Actions with no quantifiable product may be the best possible use of time. That I can sift and sort through envelopes, stacks of text and cover-weight papers in rainbow shades, quiets my mind, seals out unhelpful chatter, builds clarity. That colors lift my spirits and, I have no doubt, strengthen my immune system makes such a practice medicinal. Were I a consultant with a roster of patients, I would suggest it for healing potential.

Once we become truly quiet, I imagine John Muir among the highest branches of a Yosemite pine, we are able to hear, if not necessarily interpret, what we are trying so fervently to tell ourselves. If your message is to speed up, use big and loopy stitches, well, you have to heed that. More likely, though, it is the opposite. Our lives are not improved by doing at least two things at a time. It may seem virtuous, the very model of the Puritan ethic, and your noisesome mind will affirm it. Yet I know I am so much smarter in silence than I am in hubbub. Slow, small, quiet, deliberate. Patience, the voices murmurs, more will be revealed.

Lemony

Dispeller of shadows, a brilliant light source also warms us. It serves to remind that, against its sheer power, what lurks in dark corners will not be able to hide for long. As a color, the visual of sunshine yellow hints at its familiar taste, sweet and tangy, a favorite of the tongue. My most enduring memories of that specific citrus are the once popular giant lemon stands in the San Joaquin Valley of my childhood, usually "all you can drink" cups of ice cold, fresh lemonade, an oasis vision on a summer afternoon before cars had air conditioning.

The word "zing" often appears in the company of lemony. Rightfully so. The unmistakable color nearly fizzes with electricity, snapping us awake, bringing us back from doldrums. I have been keeping track of everyday highlights in my Hobonichi, procrastinated about designing pages for public viewing until I knew I would be able to share them. Actually, truthfully, I simply procrastinated. Enough of that, she muttered. I am called to planning by mellow yellow.

Nepenthe

The start of no other season transports me to earlier times in the same manner as summer. As Los Angeles began to swelter on Saturday, my thoughts drifted to an A&W Root Beer drive-in, oasis in Paso Robles on the vacation road back to the coast. On Sunday, when our little town was 103 at about 12:30, I recalled Nepenthe's deck above the Big Sur cliffs, our first Ambrosia Burgers with pink lemonade. I also remembered our dad telling us the meaning of "nepenthe," an ancient remedy for banishing grief, sorrow or trouble by inducing forgetfulness.

I have not gone to check my archives but suspect I write nearly the same post every year. Summer's hold on me is that tenacious and I always capitulate to its fierce, mad strength. Not to mention its ability to cloud memory.

So much to contain, all those summers, how is there room for other matters? Once I allow myself, there are multiple reveries over the light, the clothes, the movies, family vacations, Girl Scout adventures, crafts, weekly treks to the library, our series of wading pools and, best of all, free time, its own source of forgetfulness of the homework and autumn yard chores not too far distant. Until then, my sister and brother and I could count on at least one family trip that took us eventually to the sea and included restaurant meals. Pancake houses, Fisherman's Wharf, small town diners, even unfamiliar grocery stores that sold much better stuff than ours did.

More than a time of year, summer is a state of mind, one to which I happily return when prompted by changes subtle or brash. There may yet be days of our June gloom (which does not require banishing), the cooler nights, less fire-prone conditions. I suppose each of the seasons has a trickster aspect, leading us to expect its best and frequently getting conditions far different. While there are odes to every time of the year, I think summer has the edge on endurable. We can talk about rock and roll another time.

Titles

Coming up with a title for any sort of work presents an opportunity for great creative mischief. A few days before the UK and its choice filled the news, wall-to-wall, I had been thinking of a British gift for wry understatement. My classic example is Dorothy L. Sayers' Lord Peter Wimsey mystery, *The Unpleasantness at the Bellona Club.* Unpleasantness, indeed. Murder.

A theme of titles also recalls another British source, this concerning a long-term lack of clarity, for The Who song is called *Baba O'Riley* and not *Teenage Wasteland.*

Another favorite, since it arrived on the scene, is *Dr. Strangelove or: How I Learned to Stop Worrying and Love the Bomb.*

It is summer, time for reading, once a time for going to the movies where the air conditioning was free. Perhaps it is still a time for that. All of which means titles. Titles, titles and more titles. *To Think That I Saw It On Mulberry Street* or *Nancy's Mysterious Letter* or *Big Wednesday.* For years I read southern writers during the summer, heat always being a component of southern fiction. Eudora Welty's *Delta Wedding*, Carson McCullers' *The Member of the Wedding* and other works, Truman Capote's *Other Voices, Other Rooms*, Flannery O'Connor's *Wise Blood.* Whether it is true or not, I remember summer as the time of seeing westerns and the occasional epic (for the era), like *Giant.*

Making lists of things to read, things to watch is a perfectly valid summer activity. So, too, is writing a list of gifts to make for Christmas and then starting to make them. But, she whined, there is so much time and so many other things to do. In December, just remember using that as your excuse. Meanwhile, I'll be over here trying to find a version of *Earth vs. the Flying Saucers.* And taking a nap.

Camelot

My life holds moments, or longer, of Camelot. I assume we all have the experience of good we hoped would go on forever. Perhaps we knew the rarity of it, perhaps we only realized its value much later. Life being life, nothing lasts forever.

One of the matters I've pondered as we watch the O.J. Simpson documentary is how do we acquire the wisdom or maturity or generosity to know when we have been given as much of a good thing as we can reasonably hope for. How do we not push our luck or burn out struggling to hold on for just a bit more?

Any of us with an eating disorder of any duration knows how blurry the lines can become. Any of us with any addiction, ever, has needed to find such boundaries in order to survive. At the same time, we are encouraged to transcend what may be called limitations. This is considered virtuous, strong. Human existence is so full of high-wire work, balancing acts, challenges to our equilibrium. How many models can we find that let us know what is enough?

The combination of Sir Richard Burton, his (my opinion) wondrous voice and the words to what becomes a lament as Camelot wanes, fit well with the experience of aging. It is a place visited once, we have no first-hand experience there and, in spite of all we have gained over time, much of it seems to speak more fluently of loss. That this is a sobering business few can deny yet our chief assignment seems to be to find authentic joy in its midst. The only way I can attempt to walk such a confusing path is a moment at a time, a step at a time, often with lengthy pauses between.

By revising definitions, such as considering cherry-strawberry-blueberry season a Camelot of sorts, I iron some of the most grievous wrinkles out of a day. I celebrate aloud any portion of July that doesn't demand air conditioning, any night that brings untroubled, restorative sleep in abundance. I still dream of reaching some specific and personal versions of the stars, all the while giving thanks for blessings already bestowed. To have come this far with a reasonably quiet mind and the ability to wobble without falling down are no small achievements. They will do.

Cheongsam

Think antidote, distraction, diversion—the equivalent of the shiny tinfoil ball. Beauty will always save us, even when the rhetoric threatens to engulf everything. Reality will be there when we return, if we choose to.

Portals

There must be some kind of way outta here . . .

— lyrics by Bob Dylan,
as sung by Jimi Hendrix

The cupboard to Narnia, the rabbit hole, places where realities intersect or the veil thins. Are they escape hatches or entrances, or, more likely, both? Whatever assists in shoehorning us from an ordinary state to one of pure non-ordinariness becomes, by definition, a portal. Unfailingly, books meet that definition.

Since it is only July, I will probably mention it again in the next few months: summer takes me back to hours spent reading. All that uncommitted time, the wish to remain still and unsweaty, the sense of burrowing into a book and becoming invisible in the here-and-now. My son uses the word "yoink" to mean lifted, stolen, taken, filched. Books yoink me, always have, always will.

Portals: the tiny door in the base of the lamp post or between gnarled roots of a great tree, beneath a lifted rock or hidden on the ledge behind a waterfall. A car which you enter from the left, then exit on the right into an unfamiliar dimension, a transformational hat, a magic mirror, a spell, an unidentifiable key that opens an unknown lock, a never-before-noticed stairway, the stuff of magic.

In such times as these, portals become not amusements but necessities. If we stay here too long we risk being overtaken by so much that is wrong, dreadfully askew. It is only frequent escape that allows me to remain without spontaneous human combustion or melting down into a puddle of toxic dreariness. The more ways in which we can remind ourselves of vitality, of being militantly alive, the better our odds at transcending whatever would lay us low. What we seek is not permanent escape but respite. A door that allows us to find our way home again after a rejuvenating lull, that is all we need.

Light

This morning's fog burned off early from South Pasadena skies. By 7:30 or sooner it was sunny. There is a slant to morning sun, when it appears, that illuminates in the most unflattering fashion such imperfections as old lady whiskers. Yet I love it beyond cruel honesty.

While putting the theory into practice often exceeds my ability, I know I am not meant to hate, I am not meant to reject or dismiss or invest time and energy into thoughts that drain me. More than five decades ago, an excruciating time which I barely survived found me being squinted at with what I interpreted as disapproval by a psychiatrist. I felt diminished, even cursed, by his proclamation that I was, to quote, "Overly responsive to your environment." As time passed I came to see that as code for empathy.

Battered by current events, I am scarcely able to absorb what we are given as facts. If I try to speak of my interpretation with my son, my stomach hurts and things seem to spin. I have awakened in the wee hours over the past several nights and, until sleep returned, looked to PBS for whatever they were serving. Last night it was the 472,936th airing of the Dr. Wayne Dyer chronicles. Which is not to disparage Dr. Dyer in any way, just the rather bludgeoning repetition of programs on our local channel. However many times I've heard his words, the 472,936th hearing caused me to turn on a light, find my glasses, paper and pen and write things down.

"Bring happiness to all you do." Which I translated to mean don't do stuff that makes you unhappy, like rail or complain.

"See everything as miracles." No translation required.

"Practice radical humility." Even if we know we're smarter than the next guy, don't go on and on about it. And we could be wrong.

"See yourself in everyone you encounter." And I'm thinking, *ewww*, even THAT guy? Yes.

"Be strong by bending." This one I have learned. Being reminded strengthens the notion.

I can only, faintly at times, know my own truth and haven't a clue about yours. I cannot engage, least of all on social media, about the mountainous occurrences that have become our daily news. To maintain what passes for sanity, I need to become even more still and, plant-like, try to grow in the general direction of natural light. The brilliance of plants in seeking—without actual brains—what keeps them alive is a model that serves me well.

Rosy

Now numbering three, my grandnieces, Mia Rose, her big sister, Josie, and their cousin, Chili, add a warm and rosy hue to our planet simply by their presence. These girls, remarkable in myriad ways, sources of delight far beyond the circle of our family, are among the reasons why I know that bleak, dreary and threatening will not prevail.

Fear, using its best and only talent, casts a towering shadow. Its disquieting sounds on an endless loop challenge our hope and reason. But children are magic, as are music and poetry, pink, science, all great works of nature and imagination, dawn, the night sky, the Earth's creatures, the fact that somehow tomorrow continues to arrive. Magic on an infinite scale does not skimp or drag its feet, and it never gives up. Tiny Mia Rose arrived this week to remind us.

Insouciance

If we leave ourselves open to common talk, we will find these to be days full of trouble. Maintaining a state close to calm, unworried, may not be possible, insouciance unattainable. The gravitational pull of endless debate, speculation, outrage wears at the resolve to maintain quiet dignity and business as usual. As I prefer to live a peaceful life, I not only choose my battles, I sidestep them whenever possible. One reaches a certain age with no idea how many gallons remain in the tank, just how far from here one may be able to travel before the sputtering halt. I am capable of being wasteful with various resources, many of which I took for granted for too long. I am, however, clear about the finiteness of energy, emotional, mental, spiritual and physical, and wish to expend it on what/who matters. Inviting fried brain syndrome through unanswerable questions, chasing my own tail, allowing my spirits to sink under epic unpleasantness will not do.

Is there any city on the planet so associated, historically, with what is beautiful, art-filled, love-powered, glittering, intoxicating and far, far from the madding crowd as Paris? To see the dancers, some *en pointe*, satin ribbons all around shining under the Paris sky while the yards of tulle in their costumes identify them in such an unambiguous way, is to remember we have choices about how to engage with the sea of life in which we tread water. I am not unconcerned nor disconnected from the politics and future of the free world. I know I have nothing to add to the rhetoric. For reasons of preserving peace of mind I will not step into it as into battle and refuse to try and shout down anyone whose opinion differs from mine. Because it is what I wish for myself, not just on this matter but generally, I feel that all of us are entitled to our preferences, without explanation, without defense.

Experiment

In my mind, the phrase "painful trial-and-error" has repeated itself over the decades. How else do we learn? How do we discover? Life as I experience it is highly adaptive and therefore, experimental. "THIS could work," the optimist's creed.

Because catalogs persist in showing us plus-size clothing on model-size models, we order with hope in our hearts, visions of loveliness making us nearly drunk with anticipation. Reality often has different plans. If we hadn't tried, we wouldn't know.

We continue to try on this existence, that is our mission. Mary Chapin Carpenter sings of, ". . . *a life that's never safe and dry.*" So it should be. If the answers were known, why would we ever explore or step beyond the known, the tried, the relatively true? It only takes one solution to erase the discouragement of the first million attempts, or something very like that.

And in case you forgot, very little agrees to being hurried. Like, say, love.

Hold

Storage for a ship's cargo or loving arms, words and where they can run to. Hold on, hold out, to have and to hold, hold this for me, hold up.

Gravity holds us in place, yet recent displays of gymnastic excellence say this may not be true for everyone. Hold a job, foothold, toehold, behold, I wanna hold your hand. He's a holdover from the last administration.

Contain, keep, protect, ensnare, persevere, cherish. Determined, stubborn, clinging, trapped, lawless, powerless. What is this strange hold you have over me? Hypnotic, possessive, bewitching, fated. Hold my place in line, hold me in your thoughts. Reserve, guarantee, promise.

Don't put me on hold. Disregard, dismiss, ignore.

We hold these truths to be self-evident.

Part VII

Impossible things

Life against all odds. Winston Churchill told us, "Never, never, never give up." In daily matters, matters of heart and mind, expressions of spirit, stubborn refusal to take no for an answer, fingers in our ears singing "la-la-la" as we are scolded, chided and told all the reasons why not. Ha! we say. The voice of that flea, that gnat, one of our better angels in disguise, sets up a rumbling soliloquy that only we can hear, either telling us to do it anyway or to wait, wait, wait. Patience is considered a virtue for a reason.

I suppose "believe" is the operative word here. We do not dissolve in our baths. The great winds come yet we are still standing. Reversals of fortune suggest that we grow more frugal, more cautious, but never hopeless. Perhaps the opposite. I have never accepted the notion that we are tested. Life comes along wearing its ordinary-life resoled shoes and frequently washed, possibly hand-me-down unassuming and faded uniform and delivers messages good, bad and indifferent. To each of us. We are free to choose the next step. Recall all the times goodness of a most unlikely nature sat itself down on your front step, more astonished than even you, beholding its presence. Messages and their carriers are dispatched, who knows from where, and suddenly what couldn't possibly be, is. Today might be the day to run through the streets, calling "Thank you" to the animate and the inanimate. Both will understand.

Contemplated losses

On Saturday a Priority Mail package arrived from my 83-years-old stepmother. It contained a letter, some current photos of deer nibbling on everything green in her yard and an album, with this description:

> *I am sending you the enclosed because the fire at Lake Nacimiento is moving west (we smell it and sometimes see the smoke) and the folks on San Simeon Road are on evacuation alert.*
>
> *This photo album of Russ from babyhood to newspaper reporter and columnist was prepared by Russ and given to me one Christmas and I have treasured it. But my feeling is that it really belongs to you and your sibs and I would feel terrible if, in the continuing drought and very long fire seasons, Cambria might be decimated and this album destroyed.*

The album holds photos of my father, now gone nearly 22 years, that I'd never seen before, including one of a tiny fellow in a sailor-type suit, long before his naval enlistment in World War II. I wept for the words in the letter, for the pictures never seen and the faces of my brother and his son, perhaps a bit of mine, so clearly present in the serious and smiling images of my father.

As of Sunday afternoon, I have not been able to reach her by phone, will keep trying and then send off a letter in the morning if that fails. She tells of packing the car in preparation for evacuation notice, which it seems did not come. Having been through that once myself, I am familiar with the sense of unreality and terror that comes with contemplating the loss of all material goods, the notion of sanctuary and home, the always uncertain whims of weather and chance.

She mentions also, during the description of California's more than 60 million trees dead from drought and bark beetles, that the five trees she and my father planted on their hilly lot have had to be chopped down. *"The two redwoods at the foot of the driveway are turning brown,"* she says.

That she felt the need to part prematurely with Dad's gift left me without coherent words to speak into the phone on Saturday. Thinking of her on her own having to decide just what to save if word came to flee caused me to admire, not for the first time, how capable she is, how good at figuring things out.

Loss, the contemplation thereof if we must, and the memory of it, never leave us. For too many, this will be the summer of smoke, of ash, of tears. For some, it is a small, sweet-smiling boy and a book reluctantly surrendered to keep it safe. May we be good stewards of this gift.

Untamed

Not domesticated or otherwise controlled.

After a great many years and actually hearing the equivalent of *"What will the neighbors think?"* as I grew up, I am coming to a gradual and reluctant peace with being under-domesticated. There are turns of mind that simply do not adhere to rules of what some might call normal behavior. Not that I believe in normal as an existing thing. I think there is ideal, then there is pretty much everything else.

For some an untamed state may manifest with variant hair, clothing, piercings, modes of transportation, lifestyle and numerous outward signs with which I am unfamiliar. In others it may reflect more a way of thinking, of seeing, that does not quite line up with the indicated borders.

Though the dictionaries do not seem to offer it as a choice, the word "unsquelched" probably comes closer to the state which has occupied my thoughts. As squelched indicates forcefully silenced or suppressed, then its opposite would be determinedly outspoken or assertive. In short, being one's self, true, authentic.

A voice or voices within are, I believe, always urging us toward our own truths, toward the inhabiting of our authentic shapes, so to speak, not seeking camouflage as creatures less brilliant than we are, usually for the sake of others' comfort. Each of us shines with a unique light which, if dimmed, can exist no other way. The world will have to get by somehow without it, an unquantifiable loss.

Believing in the rightness, rather than the wrongness, of us being us is a source of swelling optimism. The tiniest loosening of that too-tight belt of self-squelching can free our minds, hearts and spirits. We expand, not in miserly, mincing half-steps but in a gush, a whoosh, a genie-out-of-the-bottle burst of what was too little becoming, suddenly and happily, enough. We are meant to be one with all that is wild and wonderful, big and beautiful and oh-so-bold, never to be silent and small again.

Uncommon

Plant a garden in which strange plants grow and mysteries bloom.

— Ken Kesey

Let us not be content with the ordinary, the too-familiar, the comfortably common. Let us venture a bit further afield, either in our minds or our steps, to places not-quite-known. Let us befriend the strange.

Firstly, I believe on some level that it is ALL a mystery. What do we really know? How little of what does or may exist have we actually encountered and how much remains beyond the edge of our acquaintance? Most, that is the answer.

Even within ourselves are caverns, craters of immeasurable depths. We ourselves are as the ocean, of which less than 5% has been explored. Think of it! On a day when we feel at the high end of Smarty Pants-osity, we are actually rather short of the mark, not because we are lacking but because there is so much that remains, for now, unknowable or unseen, unimagined or, at the very least, rare. Which is, you ought not to be surprised, the good news. So much to discover. The time of explorers is not behind us, don't let the history books fool you. Just this month researchers learned there are four species of giraffes, not only one as had been assumed. What other secrets are hiding in plain sight?

Mr. Kesey (of the quote above) was not one to accept much at face value, certainly not to accept it as promoted by the establishment. I hope this doesn't tilt your planet too severely, but they don't always tell us the truth and they don't always know the answer. In addition to existing mysteries, we have the power to fashion our own, to weave stories and paint pictures in which unknowns comfortably lurk.

All the most choice bits are not necessarily sitting under spotlights in display cases or showroom windows. They may have burrowed in at the bottom of the Mariana Trench or could be skulking and incognito just about anywhere. They hide within human hearts and keep life fresh with their occasional, often startling revelations. Attend well. Allow the world to surprise you, baffle you, and ultimately charm you. It is waiting to do just that.

Consistency

My two great adversaries are gravity and consistency. To turn an act into a habit is the product of focus, determination and time. Landing on the same square, as it were, with each daily leap. Letting not rain nor dark of night be a reason to slide, to neglect, to procrastinate or to be half-assed. As to gravity, I tend to drop things a lot or they leap from my grasp, plus the earth seems constantly to pull me closer. I used to be considered tall.

Somewhere, once, I read that it takes 30 days to create a habit. Oh, if only. Maybe if one is under the age of, say, 35. When one is more than twice that number, well, do the math. All I know to do is begin, and continue. I've reached a point, much as I thought it would never come to this, when the day contains too few hours for all my intentions. Certainly if what I intend is to do a thing well. And who wants a sub-par habit? I'm sure I have quite enough of those already.

The vow to self of returning to art as a daily product, not a for-sale sort of product, but a thing brought into existence in whatever form, whatever medium, is a current priority. I have not yet committed to a specific amount of time every day. I'd already be in trouble if I had. As long as it is something that I can call art, I feel successful. I have not betrayed myself. Whew. As I have said many times before, if it were easy, everyone would do it.

So a day becomes parcels, liked packed lunches.

On different days, the portions of each habit-in-the-making vary in size. Too much consistency goes against my basic nature. Perhaps it needs to be a dual word week—consistency and balance, with each day allowed to bring its own set of circumstances, to set its own schedule. The fact that the world seems to see rigid consistency as more virtuous than flexible consistency is one of those slippery places. I don't do rigid well. I don't do rigid at all. And thus, the challenge.

On the other hand, a day full of bento boxes would not be the worst thing. I could reclaim time spent cooking and use it for art or serenity or stretching. Meanwhile, we, as they say, start where we are with what we have and do what we can. One can do no more.

Mucilage

These are days, it seems, to think about what exactly IS the glue that holds us together, either to maintain a congruity with self or a plural binding of one to another. There is something, beyond gravity, centripetal force, magnets, chewing gum or baling wire, that stops us from dissolving into fragments. Its forms are as numerous as are we who rely on its existence.

At its most exalted it is sticky and honey-sweet, with names like optimism, kindness, beauty, and love. It is scent, known to transport us in memory to other realms and times, or words, as used by poets to translate, impossibly, the ineffable into language. It is color or form that jars the heart. It is magic, mostly unintentional, the product of man or nature simply bringing forth what must be brought.

It is experiences shared, even if known in solitude. It is recognition of me in you. It is music, sounds raised in thanksgiving or lament. Perhaps beyond all else it is music.

If I understand anything of the universe, it is this: we are not meant to be divided nor to seek or invent ways that make us unalike. We survive with each other, it is how we will thrive. Our hands reach out to comfort. With vocabulary we soothe and support. In the rock-hard moments we remind one another that there are softer times.

We are the glue, aided by the wonders amid which we sometimes flounder, wonders which lift our spirits, replenish our hope. There is no wonder too small or obscure to be considered medicinally adhesive. It only requires—demands—the ability to illuminate what has been dimmed. Circumstances have been known to abandon us in dark caves and haunted houses of the mind. For me, the image of a rose, bodies of water from a puddle to a fountain, canal, river or ocean, the thought and, one hopes, the taste of dark chocolate, works of art, a hummingbird outside the window, the voice of a loved one or even sight of their name reach out to frightened and lost parts of myself. They secure me to a greater circle where light prevails.

This is a gummy business and we serve as human fly paper to one another. As we abide, fastened, we joke, we sing, we listen, we doze. Our thoughts may wander but we, it is hoped, do not. We are tethered for the long ride. That is what's real. Anything else is the illusion.

Fervent

Yes, "*completely baked*" as spoken by Benjamin in *The Graduate* would qualify as fervent. Definitely feverish.

Fervent is never half-baked, never tepid, never neither-this-nor-that. It is passionate, fiery hot, may appear obsessive. Heartfelt.

What is the point of showing up with indifference? Let them talk. "*She seemed, well, awfully intense. I'm not sure that is considered good manners.*" Probably not. This is life we're talking about. As Mary Oliver says, "*your one wild and precious life.*" Be a shame to get over-excited about that and all the wonders it contains. Perhaps I need to sit back down with a cool cloth to my forehead.

As I write this, we are having oddly balmy winds, none of the chance of showers forecast as late as this morning, and the neighborhood Amazon parrots are shrieking through the skies as though warning us of something. They do a lot of jabbering so we don't take them seriously. The point is that I sit at my table on the second floor, amid the trees where I can see no cars nor dwellings. An hour ago a crow with a wingspan of several feet found delicacies in the palm tree just beyond my window. His departure sounded like an old window shade that had been yanked down, then let go to flap and shudder.

Rilke knew that our ordinary moments are filled with texture, brilliance, joy, sorrow, sights and events to make our hearts leap or thud. Best to take nothing for granted, to see it all as miraculous for the everyday is our most intimate universe, the room in which we spend the most time, the place it all happens. Even peak events are cushioned by the everyday. It is that with which we most surely need to fall in love, if we have not. I had a stamp made that says, "*Fall in love with everything,*" then I realized there are some situations in which that is difficult, many in fact, but as a goal, an aspiration, it seems a not bad fit. I use the word love more and more, realizing that I do love so much. I do, in loud and giddy and probably unladylike ways. The list is longer every day.

I occasionally visit the Jet Pens website, perhaps to look at bottled inks. Some of the colors, with names like Apache Sunset, Heart of Darkness or Dragon Catfish Pink, make me think of fervent correspondence. Is there really any other kind?

Choreography

First, credit to Jerome Robbins for conception and choreography of *West Side Story*. The opening sequence has never lost its appeal, likely never will.

This week's word came to me while watching the Golden State Warriors play the New Orleans Pelicans the other night. Having seen the Warriors throughout last season, including the playoffs and championship, I had a picture of what the court looked like during a game. With the addition of Kevin Durant to the equation, it appeared to me that a new configuration was being eased into, one with which those concerned had not yet become fully fluent. Where there had once been two principles, now there were three. As one of the color commentators seemed ready to declare a team misfire part-way into the second game of the season, I saw the working out of new choreography. When you go *here*, then you go *there* and you'll be ready for *this*. Places, everyone. Rehearsals have just begun.

I find that flux influences my days, flexibility and improvisation are required if one is to keep on one's feet, even figuratively. It is still choreography, whether or not one is actively mobile. Colliding with other dancers, with fixed objects, with change, happens. Would that it happened less rather than more. We have our routines, our expectations, the pieces of the production on which we depend—our own strength, our wits, our capabilities, all of them mutable. Aging may bring these variations, this need to regroup regularly, into sharper focus, yet I know they've always been there for me. A more youthful elasticity may have masked their constancy, whereas they now step boldly from the wings and demand a place on the stage. The other dancers rearrange themselves with as much grace as they can muster. They are learning not to grumble.

It seems my actions are all variations on working to make peace with uncertainty. The phrase, "What fresh hell is this?" is one I utter often. Not hell, exactly, but still surprising, unexpected. I think of walls, the bricks hold their integrity while the mortar crumbles. How to keep it all from falling down.

As words escape me, awareness seems easier to access. It may be the product of greater stillness or the brain teaching itself new tricks. A definition of evolution refers to, "the gradual development of something, especially from a simple to a more complex form." I don't believe it was ever truly easy, we just let ourselves be fooled into thinking it so. My wish: the ability to evolve as the situation requires. There will be new steps to learn tomorrow.

Witness and remember

I'll be aroun' in the dark. I'll be everywhere-wherever you look. Wherever there is a fight so hungry people can eat, I'll be there. Wherever there is a cop beatin' up a guy, I'll be there . . . I'll be in the way kids laugh when they're hungry and they know supper's ready. An' when our folk eat the stuff they raise an' live in the houses they build—why, I'll be there.

— from *The Grapes of Wrath*
by John Steinbeck

In every way that is humanly possible, we are, I believe, intended to be present for each other, present in kindness, in love, in compassion, in support, in care, in listening, in holding with and to what is most sacred.

I am an old hippie at heart. Before the hippies appeared, I clung to the notion of being a baby beatnik. These were and are my people. I will never not cry when Henry Fonda makes that speech to his Ma during those desperately hard times. Whether or not he survives being one who continues to speak up to authority, he knows his witnessing, his naming, his presence will live on.

On Sunday, my brother Mike shared Gandalf's (J.R.R. Tolkien's) words from *The Lord of the Rings*:

> *Some believe it is only great power that can hold evil in check, but that is not what I have found. It is the small everyday deeds of ordinary folk that keep the darkness at bay. Small acts of kindness and love.*

We are extraordinary ordinary people in possession of wisdom and strength. We are healers and helpers, mourners, visionaries and heroes. We are the answer to any question, or we are capable of being such. We may, in some moments, feel as though we've lost our way. We have not. We have each been chosen to know, to witness and remember. Let us not forget.

Fear and loathing

Saturday night, while watching an episode of Anthony Bourdain's show set in London, we saw Ralph Steadman at work in his studio and sharing a meal with Bourdain. I realized my unexpectedly despairing, delayed reaction to Tuesday's election results might have been assuaged if Hunter Thompson were still here to tell us what really happened. That is a story we will likely never know and certainly not as it might have been translated through the mind of Dr. Thompson, whose possibly best-known quote tells us, "*When the going gets weird, the weird turn pro.*" It has officially gotten weird. What none of us knows is what to do next.

About *Fear and Loathing on the Campaign Trail '72*:

> *Thompson should be recognized for contributing some of the clearest, most bracing and fearless analysis of the possibilities and failures of American democracy in the past century.*
>
> — Chicago Tribune

Part of the item description from the bookseller, The BiblioFile in Gladstone, Michigan, says:

> *The best, the fastest, the hippest and the most unorthodox account ever published of the US government's presidential electoral process in all its madness and corruption. In 1972 Hunter S. Thompson, the creator and king of Gonzo journalism, covered the US presidential campaign for Rolling Stone magazine alongside the establishment newsmen of Washington. The result is a classic piece of subversive reportage and a fantastic ride on the rollercoaster of Hunter's uniquely savage imagination. In his own words, written years before Watergate: 'It is Nixon himself who represents that dark, venal and incurably violent side of the American character almost every other country in the world has learned to fear and despise.*

Walking the narrow path

Some years ago a friend told of a question asked by her husband when she was in the throes of a ta-do. He asked, "Would you rather be right or would you rather be happy?" She chose, as I did and do, happy. Every time.

We are, as a country and a planet, in a place of deep turmoil. One of the things I know beyond any doubt is that my words will not change anyone's mind, nor will theirs change mine. I forgot for a moment the truth of that. It was an uncomfortable reminder. Discord has no place in my life. I simply do not believe in arguing, in feuds, in estrangements, in being at odds with those I love or even like. I've learned through years of stress-induced ills and infirmities that fighting is very bad for my health. It weakens the immune system, erases a quiet mind and produces only grief. It steals sleep and the ability to trust in a good outcome.

I also don't believe that hate is an appropriate word to apply to other living things, least of all to my fellow humans. Disagreement needs to include tolerance, the forbearing of hate-filled exchanges, of baiting, demeaning, ridiculing, insulting, oppressing, bullying. It is unreasonable to expect to hold the moral high ground when one is spouting venom, no matter how perfume-drenched it may be.

I do not feel we are required to explain ourselves to others. I believe all are entitled to the dignity of choice, for which we each have very personal reasons, strongly held ideas.

It is a narrow path, trying to walk through this mine field, not staying neutral but maintaining what I hope can be a respectful silence. My voice added to the din would only make it louder. I hear of families so divided they cannot sit together at the Thanksgiving table, detente a distant illusion. My immediate family, never exactly large, has dwindled. Its members are too rare and precious, our years here growing too short to treat recklessly in the election's aftermath. A harmonious life is hard-won, not by abandoning our truths but by asking them to sit quietly in the back seat for the duration of the ride.

When in doubt

In times of confusion, I turn or have turned variously to food, sleep, humor, dithering, weeping, growing quiet, snapping, any distraction like organizing my color pencils yet again, pondering and, as a last resort, making a very simple plan.

The holidays confuse me. Relentless promoting of costly, material goods makes me sad. It seems so anti-holiday. I used to be able to participate so differently, certainly with greater energy and other resources. That was a very long time ago. What passes for The News confuses me for I mistrust most of it, either to be actually newsworthy or to be true.

While I would not call myself a tough cookie of the old school, neither am I easily confused so it takes a really large and seething mass of chaos to throw me any distance. Also known as, when the holidays and news collide.

A useful response to confusion is not unlike a healthy reaction to physical peril from, oh, a poisonous snake or other predatory, lethal life form. For me, that means stand still for as long as necessary. Do nothing big or noisy or fast. Drawing, with or without coloring, fits that description. When figures or forms seem too much, I draw words, often silly ones that somehow help me feel less disoriented. As each of us is unique, what is medicine for one may be further confusion for another. It is not one size fits all.

I freely admit to being a conspiracy theorist. One of the suspected conspiracies involves someone/someones somewhere being highly invested in keeping us confused or distracted in ways that render us non-functioning. This is not new business, this didn't just happen. Our job is to be as present, as bright and alert as possible, as don't-get-fooled-again skeptical as we can be. Getting caught up with all the other fish who swim around in circles renders us useless.

It doesn't matter how one combats this fugue state, just that we resist it. There IS a way out. It is our job to find it, to draw its picture so we'll know it when/if it shows up again, regardless of the disguise it chooses. Each of us is responsible for being present, for being our truest and most solid self by our own definition. There is much to be said for simply holding a place of certainty when doubt seems to have the upper hand. It is not about being right, it is about being.

Stars

For our Christmas program in the 6th grade, I got to be in the glee club. I have no memory of how that happened, just that it was the vehicle to learning Christmas carols beyond those we sang in Sunday School. We even learned two different tunes for "Away In A Manger" and I still remember them both. Impossible yet true.

Suns, moons, cats and stars are among my favorite subjects for doodles and drawing. The fact of stars assures me we will never unravel all the great mysteries, which comforts me enormously.

Carl Sagan said this of us:

> *The nitrogen in our DNA, the calcium in our teeth, the iron in our blood, the carbon in our apple pies were made in the interiors of collapsing stars. We are made of star stuff.*
>
> — from *Cosmos*

Stars and songs make a potent team. To sing, or play, of stars positions them in the firmament, their rightful home. John Fahey's guitar, "We Three Kings."

The holiday season, of which all that shines brightly is a great part, is nearly upon us. Candles, tinsel, lights, stars, the winter nights less dark for their warm glow, no matter how near or far.

Engage

I feel as though I do a poor job of explaining myself when called upon to do so. That is probably because I believe we should not be asked to explain ourselves. Years and years ago I realized I would never find words precise enough to say who I am to someone who couldn't or didn't want to know.

A recent conversation with my most capable, kind and interested nurse practitioner about why it was my priority to re-establish too-long neglected drawing as a daily habit before moving on to doing the same with chair yoga backed me into that corner of trying to say why this was so. A few days later it came to me that art generally is how I engage with the world. Writing, images—either my own or borrowed from the internet—are my voice when not conversing one-to-one. How I am in and of the wider world is better expressed through essays or fiction, through the work of my own hand or photos of what has meaning for me. The conundrum of how to be known without explaining. The long and short-term benefits of a chair yoga practice are not lost on me. However beneficial, though, they take a backseat to an act which carries me outwardly forward while inwardly grounding me more firmly as myself.

This is, you realize, my process. It may not match yours, nor does it need to. Had the internet not been invented, had no platform been offered for creating a free daily (or less often) written musing on any topic I chose, I could easily be, if such a thing still goes on, in downtown Los Angeles' Pershing Square shouting my truths at passing cars and uneasy pedestrians. I could be pressing leaflets into their hands rather than having professional representation for my snowmen, cats, cupcakes, roses, suns, moons, flowers and citizens through rubberstamp companies that turn my drawings into product and send them/me forth.

That I am *here* for a reason I accept as fact. What I interpret as the reason may shift, may adjust itself with circumstances though it never strays far from a notion of service in the form of that which brings more light than it takes. We've no idea how long we have to complete our assignment, as though we ever could, and I feel some urgency about doing what I think of as my work better, more fully even at my decidedly slowed pace. I can only be here, part of my own support staff, in so many ways on any given day. I swear chair yoga is next. Meanwhile, there is lettering to practice and pages to fill.

Make things

My sister, brother and I grew up following the model of a mother who made things. She was a fine arts major and everything, including the elementary school newsletter, became art in her hands. I have a faint but I believe accurate memory of one of her newsletters, featuring patterns for Three Little Pigs finger puppets. She launched us each on a lifetime path of creating, each according to our specific muses. Music, sports cars, carpentry, cooking, building, sewing, retail display, vintage fashion and accessories, drawing, coloring, paper craft, writing, my siblings and I continue to expand and explore the places our minds and hands can take us.

When fully immersed in the doing, I find it impossible to think other thoughts. Existence in the moment shrinks to the point of a pencil, the heft of the scissors, the accuracy of glue placement. It is another world, the realm of alchemy. We are transformed, returned eventually to ordinary life, perhaps with the ability to see it through new eyes.

In a Facebook post a few days ago, Dr. Clarissa Pinkola Estes, sharing a video of extravagant, traditional tulip-pattern cookies, said this: *"I often think of this in our fast food world, and HAIL! to the cooks and bakers. I find you to be HOLY people who bless others with your daily works. Thank you!"*

All that remains for you to do is GO. Go to your studio, your garage, your kitchen, your garden, your shop, your factory and make stuff. It is never too early, it is never too late. Go. Now.

Sister and brother

I use the word Christmas rather than holidays for it was Christmas that my family celebrated. It is our tradition. It is the past to which I return this time every year. It is my personal version of the Twilight Zone where I know it will be the mid-1950s, where my sister will be around five or six years old, my brother around eight or nine, and I somewhere between 10 and 12. When our mother isn't looking, we will make compressed balls of the tinsel and toss them at the tree, rather than draping it strand by strand as she instructed. When the lights are on, we will lie on the floor with our heads beneath the branches, and let our wishing minds carry us away.

The three of us have spoken as adults of the brief interlude, perhaps only one year or at the most two, when our mother sought the short-cut of what we called the Ready-Pack Christmas stocking. A dime store standard of scratchy red mesh with a festive, stapled image atop a bag of, well, stuff. We were used to receiving one of our father's socks with a splendid orange in the toe and a handful of personally selected treasures to open in the middle of the wakeful night. We fussed terribly about the indignity of it, though the Ready-Pack gave us a lasting tradition: the Chinese finger trap, ever after one of Santa's constants.

They say that the act of recalling an event changes our memory of it. Physics may one day prove that remembering can alter the event itself. What I know is that, among all the joys that Christmas continues to bring to my life, the most enduring times, the ones etched most deeply into my heart, my very core, are the ones when Laurie, Mike, and I were young together, almost swallowed whole like Jonah by the impossible magic of those days.

Why not fiction?

On Christmas Eve, with very little time, I tried to write a follow-up story with the characters introduced at Halloween of 2015. I had pleasing photos for illustration, showing dolls by artist Sandy Mastroni which had inspired the original piece. I had a blurry idea of the shape I wanted the story to take, elements I wanted to include. After a couple hours it was as weighty as an anchor and all I could do was put it aside until either the story or I managed to lighten up. Still waiting.

On Facebook today, a friend mentioned the challenge of naming characters in fiction, with useful suggestions added to the comment thread, reminding me I have novel-length work *just sitting there*. That seems to leave me adding Fiction Reworking to my list of Stuff I Would Like to Turn Into Habit. I've discussed the Chair Yoga, plus working with hand weights, plus Art Every Day or So Help Me. Then there's the fact of a daily nap not being an option but a necessity. All this may require me to become more serious about time, about where the boundaries are. Seeing things blocked out, in my planner, for instance, is not my norm. As with time generally, I tolerate, actually welcome, its fluid aspects as I experience them. But I doubt that sort of relationship gets books written.

So. There IS no reason why there can't be fiction. I assume if there can be little fiction, there might be big fiction. What was unthinkable yesterday becomes a possibility today. The universe as I have come to know it is fluent in encouragement. It rubs its galactic palms together at the thought of surprising us with our own most deeply held desires, seeming to wander, whistling, through the neighborhood as we write an episode here, a chapter there, thinking of them as short-short stories. As we humans tend to be greater than the sum of our parts, perhaps the same is true of building a novel using the model of the Add-A-Pearl necklace.

It is a daunting word, novel. For now, I may speak of my Add-A-Pearl necklace. We will know what I mean.

January

I believe January is one of those hybrids, both month and state of mind. As I age, I find that I am happier with more hours of sunlight, more warmth. While I expect that, come August, I will be displeased with temperatures above 105, there is more day to the days. Winter nights, relieved by strings of cheery, glowing bulbs, are bearable. Without them, a sense of isolation creeps in. Shivering, along with watery gray skies, aggravates a nature already listing toward occasional melancholy. And all of this, mind you, takes place in Southern California, not North Dakota or even Virginia where winter doesn't kid around. And, may I add, how much I have always loved the rain. Just a bit less so when it falls in January.

January can feel like a primitive rope bridge strung between the sweetness, the natural or induced jollity of Christmas and the once-celebrated heart-filled red joy of Valentine's Day. Thank you, Dr. King, for giving us a holiday mid-month to release some of the chilly tension.

As I see each day as the chance for a new beginning, the New Year holds no particular promise of transformation to come. December brings a unique shine, associated with stars and glitter, colorful packaging, specific music, greetings exchanged, good wishes, peace on earth. January is the absence of festivity, all possible childlike anticipations too far away to give comfort. If one could find a way to spread the holidayness of December a bit thinner, to stretch it beyond the first of the year rather than using it up in what feels like a week or even just the one day, I believe winter would lose some of its sting. One would feel less bereft. No doubt you are thinking that to make the celebration of December holidays a more lengthy endeavor would dilute them. I disagree. January needs a little Christmas or its own special not-Christmas, its own bit of happy gleam to chase the deepened shadows, the damp, the ice.

I am not glum as I sit typing in my red sweater having spritzed cautiously frugal dots of Chanel #5 so the fragrance wafts from wrists to stuffy nose, singing to the senses. Without inflated expectations of Christmas, I no longer experience the droop that used to follow. Still, January at best is a wet blanket, at worst a bleak expanse. No, it is not a particularly rational response to a collection of days that mean no harm but one's response to stimuli is rarely rational. Keep the fires burning, hibernate if that helps pass the time, fill the hours with laughter and all that feeds the senses. Press on. Always know that something wonderful IS just around the corner. Hello, February. Will you be my winter Valentine?

Sunshine

While I often label color as a nutrient, I know beyond doubt that sunshine actually is. A vitamin D deficiency smartens one up rather quickly to the fact that a human body needs the light of the sun. In my world that leaves color the task of being sunshine for the spirit.

It is not alone in its assignment, for I corral it with its fellows, including beauty by multiple definitions, swiftly running rivers, things that smell wonderful, the love of and for friends and family, silliness, kindness, insight and intelligence, artfully arranged words. Oh, such a long list. For the spirit to be underfed requires cataclysm of epic proportions.

I have long believed that any garment ought to have pockets and to be without them is a failure of aesthetics and duty. In those pockets one can keep and transport the necessary charms, talismans, symbols of spiritual sunshine, available like smelling salts when weariness gains the upper hand.

We have never truly known where the next step of our journey will take us. That we don't know today only suggests there may be additional reasons for gathering to us more closely that which brightens and enlivens, that which lifts our hearts. Vitality fuels our imaginations, empowers and strengthens. The world needs us, needs our spirits, inspired, nourished, hopeful and strong. The world needs, we need, our sunshine.

Attend

Multiple decades of living have schooled me. They have enlightened and confused and guided me, taught me to recognize the urgings from which my truth emerges. I have learned, I continue to learn, to attend my soul's guidance.

My mother once told me that when I tried to lie I lit up like a tilt sign. While I knew in the moment she intended to discourage further attempts at dishonesty, I also believed her. While the blaring of a flashing tilt sign may be more internal now than it was then, it is no less present, certainly no less emphatic.

While we find companionship and support in numbers, in reality we always ride alone. In certain respects each of us is an army of one, directed on a unique assignment. Adhering to my own truth while legions would have me join and follow can be isolating. Worse, it may cause me to doubt what I have come to know as my path. It seems part of what we are here to be is misunderstood, for it is impossible, not to mention onerous, trying to explain a state so clear when viewed within and so limp and inadequate-appearing when held to the light of day and critical eyes. We want those who care for us to understand, to trust our self-knowing, realizing they may not.

What any of us is best equipped to do is be our self. To be that we must first know just what that means. Arriving at that information is a lengthy, possibly lifelong process. Such awareness is hard-won, its value unquestionable. We navigate our days amid the noise of many voices. Know the one that speaks to and for you with the greatest honesty and attend to that.

Cheering up the sick people

My maternal grandmother was a battlefield nurse in World War I. When, in her 60s, she became ill she was admitted to the Veteran's Hospital in West Los Angeles. Long before freeways went from Pasadena to those far reaches, my father drove our family over one night a week so my mother and I could visit her. Dressed in my Easter suit, I passed for the minimum age allowed to call on patients. On one of our visits, she was not in her bed nor anywhere to be found around the ward. No one could tell us where she might be. We were apprehensive, as she was nearly blind and had recently lost a leg to diabetes. We waited beside her bed as they screened a movie for the women. I think it was something with Elvis Presley.

Eventually an attendant wheeled her back and I'm sure we hissed our questions at her, trying not to talk over the movie. *Where have you been? We were so worried.* Etc. Her calm response was, "*I've been out cheering up the sick people.*"

I think of her often, as I knew her and as the young Gertrude Holden of Boston, sailing to France after graduating nursing school at what was then Peter Bent Brigham Hospital. In addition to "*cheering up the sick people*," she was known to have said on numerous occasions, "*It isn't Boston but it IS Massachusetts,*" both of which I have borrowed and quoted all my adult life, probably to the annoyance of those who have listened to me the most.

The thought of her, of her ability to find something of value in what to many of us would seem worthless, the model she was that told me no matter what, if we draw breath we have something to offer others, helps me at times when I begin to sag or doubt. If we are without words, we can listen. We can offer a hand to hold. We can refuse to be discouraged. We can whistle, we can sing, we can be very clear about what matters most, about what is our truth.

I know that hospital ward, which once felt so cavernous, which I would swear reached into distant and shadowy corners on our night visits, would no longer appear so large. I remember the relief my mom and I felt as we caught sight of her, seeming to return again from the battlefields, from very far away, her face, her spirit beaming. I hope some of her lives on in me.

A widened mind

A closed mind in a hamster wheel, a spinning treadmill from which I would never escape IF I stayed there without allowing in light, air and other possibilities. I can suffocate myself with narrow, pinched thinking. I, and I assume many of us, am not the best judge of my better aspects. Too often I fail to find any finer points when I bolt the doors, pull the blackout curtains and burrow into my obvious and plentiful, as I believe, shortcomings. This happens most often under stress and when tired.

With some rather limited experience of meditation, I know how a quiet mind feels, what it says—or doesn't say. The agitated mind is a liar, perhaps out of malice, perhaps simply from fatigue. It, in my case, has compiled evidence of insufficiency in pretty much all areas. Viewing the documents in the case, my spirits sag lower still. The evidence is so compelling.

But wait! Put the focus elsewhere, like, say, sinking into an interesting movie or book, seeing the world with a refreshed perspective. It actually feels as though louvers have opened in my temples, allowing refreshing breezes in, letting stale notions escape, certainly thinning the noxious gasses they produce. With a brain open to the winds and the world, I feel so much more connected to all that is not me. I gain a sense of being part of a vast and benevolent entity in which good thoughts prevail, in which "thank you" becomes a mantra, in which unseen hands are joined in fellowship.

A widened mind is not so much the product of being really smart as it is about being open. I thrive on ideas that are not just self-generated. Like when somebody forgets to change the water in the fish bowl, things grow slimy, murky and, let's face it, deadly. I remind myself, or outside forces remind me, to unlatch the windows, to grab the broom and sweep away sour opinions. Perfection is neither a reasonable nor attainable goal, but expanded thinking is, a practice that lets me see myself as more than I seem. We are here to be, I believe, the best versions of ourselves, something we find through being connected to each other and the infinite in which we dwell.

Inner creatures

Various sources tell us of our inner beings, the ways they inform and shape our lives. Inner goddesses, the inner child, inner chef, inner entrepreneur. I wish for us each to claim our inner creatures.

My creatures are closely tied to the inner child, their gifts the ones I wish she'd had to provide a greater sense of safety and of self. My inner octopus, a master of camouflage and squeezing into tiny hiding places. Tentacles, essentially eight additional brains, would have sensed when conditions required caution. I cannot imagine an octopus behaving recklessly. My outer child/teenager was a puzzling combinations of timid and foolhardy. The creature's ability to move swiftly yet with the languid grace found in water-dwellers speaks to my inner mermaid. The sense of becoming weightless, certainly less gravity-dominated in water still calls to me.

My inner bear, considered a light hibernator, enjoys long winter naps while being able to awaken and take part in Christmas festivities and a winter birthday, neither of which require actually getting dressed. An especially thick, warm bathrobe could transition handsomely between cave and civilization and would, of course, have roomy pockets to carry foraged treats back to the nest. There might also be an inner tortoise capable of hibernating more deeply. The three which were family pets spent their winters in a well-protected location packed with dry leaves, hibernation by concierge.

There is probably a spot at which a spirit animal and inner creature intersect. The attributes of totem forms supply what we most need: a moth, a crow, a fish and my most frequent visitors, parrots. We live in one of the Southern California neighborhoods inhabited by flocks of wild Amazon parrots. They roost and cavort just outside our windows. At times their squawking drowns out conversation. We invent dialogue for them, their loud exchanges sounding like accusation and complaint.

For at least the past 10 years or so I have identified with the story of *Ferdinand the Bull*, realizing that my activity of greatest comfort is a metaphoric smelling of the flowers, sidestepping conflict, declining to engage in rivalries, feuds, stink talk in general. With the goal of a quiet mind and quiet heart, I follow Ferdinand's example, growing still as I celebrate beauty wherever I find it.

Tiptoe

My thought for the week: I'd rather not walk where I feel the need to tiptoe. I am at home in art, in beauty, in poetry, color, music, laughter, all foods for the senses. I find strength there, bedrock wisdom, grounding. For whatever life has planned, I am better for leaning into what provides enduringly solid footing while acting as a timeless balm for my soul.

Wholeness

In cultures other than mine there are ceremonies to restore balance, refit missing pieces into the spaces left by their exodus. My absence from self has been an itinerary of comings and goings for which no estimated times of arrival or departure were known.

Before poetry—appreciated and even studied long ago but not absorbed, not inhaled, no door opened wide enough for habitation, accommodating the bulky goods with which it travels—caught me, I assumed that my once-absent segments had all flown home. Now I find that what I took for life in full measure was more a silhouette. Poetry has a way of poking its fingers into vacant corners, eyebrows raised with the question, shouldn't there be something *here*?

Poetry, if it wanted to, could beat any self-help manual senseless. A poem is a far more believable testimonial: I survived to write this. Poetry doesn't tell you, it shows you. How is it that, over not so many months, a literary form, an art, has become teacher, guide, source of wisdom and the voice that keeps me awake at night (in a good way)? Painful shards of memory that used to steal my breath now look like *material.*

There is study ahead, there is travel. My fragments could turn up anywhere. They arrive in daily emails, my heart lurching in recognition. They emerge in posts and comments, they step shyly forward from links that have a telling glimmer: look here.

In a culture thought by some to be without shamans we are not lost or abandoned. The poets rattle and drum, they chant and dance. We are redeemed by words, their incantations point the way.

Incomplete

I look at the art of Stephane Dauthuille, the heads or limbs of his richly-gowned women existing just outside the paintings' edges, and I do not wonder what is missing. I have no feeling that what these works say to me is an incomplete message. They speak fully. We are each allowed to interpret as we will.

The notion of a life in which nothing essential is missing is relatively new to me. Any of us of moderate means is capable of wishing for material goods or circumstances that could, we believe, make everything better. Depending on your definition of better.

A heart or mind that chases after the unattainable allows a sense of lack to cast shadows on what actually IS, obscuring, diminishing what we have. Contentment is not a product of merely having but of the awareness of and gratitude for what is present. As I write this, it sounds simplistic. Of course, everyone knows that, I chide myself. I can't say that I've always known it.

As the only story I can tell fully is my own and though I may write "we," what I mean is me/I. Historically, my greatest sense of incompleteness involves my relationship with myself, with a notion of insufficiency in every nameable category. Becoming our authentic selves, allowing that to be not only enough but desirable requires such traits as acceptance, faith/trust, the willing suspense of doubt and continually reviewing the situation.

I assume of others as I do of myself that we are all works in progress. I once believed that meant an endless striving to be somehow better than I was. I had no idea there could be something succulent about being miraculously ordinary, ordinary meaning just me being me. To be fully who we are, treasuring that profound and unique state without apology or asterisks to indicate missing parts, ah, there's a challenge. Within the boundaries of human life with its sorrows, we seem to have the option of being not only happy but complete. When our mother passed, my sister described her as dancing in heaven with her mother, now restored to two good legs. In the realm of spirit, measured by the heart, I believe I have what I need, two good legs and a great deal more.

Have I told you lately that I love you?

My family of origin was not much for saying, *"I love you."* I actually cannot remember it being said to me or among the five of us as my sister, brother and I were growing up. We siblings say it now, yes we do. The words are spoken between me and my friends, me and my son. Anyone who reads this blog or any Facebook posts knows that I love lots. Lots of people, things, weather, states of being, colors, creatures and love itself. I had a rubber stamp made, small, simple, that urges, "*Fall in love with everything.*"

I was already thinking of this phrase for Word of the Week when last night I dreamed—for about the nine-hundred-and-forty-seven-thousandth time—of an old beau. In the dream I had to turn down an invitation to be his date at a car show, his yellow dream Chevrolet beckoning, as I was already going with someone else. The someone else said, "*You know how much he's in love with you, don't you?*"

My answer was, "*Yes, but he won't do anything about it.*" (Please excuse me for I know the dreams of other people are generally tedious.) The dream caused me to ponder more than four decades speckled with memorable, treasured blurts of affection. We are not growing younger, just like the rest of you. I grapple with the still-adolescent parts of my mind that think saying those words to a man who has been a friend, uniquely, to me for more than half my life has to be "*going somewhere.*" What a twit I can be. It has always been somewhere, everywhere. It is a gift, as my sister might say, "*A pearl beyond price,*" to have people we love, even better but not required if they love us back.

Gift

I assume we each retain possession of a child's delight upon receiving a gift, especially when it arrives as a surprise. What a bonanza this week when a friend sent not only the newest version of the *Flow Book for Paper Lovers* (300 pages of paper-paper-and more paper, the subject of a future post) and her copy of *Sowa's Ark*, a collection of creatures which inhabit the imagination of German artist Michael Sowa.

Thank you, Elaine, for the multi-part joy, first the arrival, then the opening and now the ongoing enjoyment of the rich contents. In my family, we called such surprises "Hi presents." Thoughtful, generous and such fun to receive.

Spirit encounters

Spiritual practices help us move from identifying with the ego to identifying with the soul. Old age does that for you too. It spiritualizes people naturally.

— Ram Dass

Ram Dass also said, *"Treat everyone you meet like God in drag."*

I have come to believe that all encounters, human and otherwise, are spirit encounters. Human to human, it is far too easy to slip into expectations, anticipating certain outcomes, making no allowance for the fact of spirits meeting—or colliding—and instead simply reacting.

Beneath the exterior, applied selves we may fashion to carry our often vastly different spirits from place to place are the grottoes, the hidey-holes where we truly live. Spaces secret and safe where there is no reason to be other than who we are. However deeply hidden, we are always at home within. It feels wildly essential to me that I try and remember this, remember that we and our exchanges occupy sacred ground, the conversations beneath, behind the spoken words.

I wonder after a night of vivid dreaming in which all visitors feel so present, whether others share that experience. There have been far too many of these dreams for me not to believe they, too, are spirit encounters. People long departed or perhaps merely distant arrive and I awake knowing we have spent those dreaming moments, during which much is always revealed, together. There is a sense of needing to send spirit emissaries to communicate without disguise or armor, that this is the only realm in which such honesty can occur. That I am capable of imagining these dreams are more than dreams I freely acknowledge, yet I know myself to be capable of recognizing the existence of unlikely events, of trusting what cannot be verified.

In spite of loss, pain, terror and occasional defeat, life is the on-going seance during which we become familiar with magic. As I've been typing, Hummingbird has visited my window twice, checking to see that amnesia hadn't overtaken me, confirming that I continue as a student of its message of joy, lightness and love shared.

A memory of magic

As young children, my brother and I had imaginary friends. His were both named Robert. Mine were named for three of my mother's college sorority sisters. They stopped by for tea. Our sister didn't play with imaginary friends, but had a stuffed bear named Elmira who alternately received rejection slips and checks from magazine publishers. There were days when the family junk mail held nothing for her, then there would be a check and our congratulations. Once in a while a manuscript was returned and we carried on as if nothing had happened.

Looking back on our fantasy play, I see us as children into whose lives a great big handful of magic beans had fallen. It is beyond my knowing, whether we created alternate worlds to escape the ordinary one or our make-believe was simply a product of being children, particularly children of parents who were also well connected to imagination, expressed through their writing and art and day-to-day living.

As we grew, our lives expanded when messengers of real magic began to appear. Some of them were drawn by our father's newspaper column or the radio talk shows on which he was interviewed as an expert on flying saucers.

It was through this door that Jackie and Sandy walked. A retired couple, they spent their summers traveling through North America with a carnival, he doing card tricks and she telling fortunes. They also loved the desert, a passion shared with our dad, and Jackie had seen UFOs. They became our godparents in non-ordinary reality and made our back-country desert trips much livelier with their tales of carney life, successful unearthing of ghost town relics and their unshakable belief in things which could not be explained.

Dad's column led to our meeting an actual, larger-than-life treasure hunter named Romaine who traveled alone into the jungles of Mexico and South America looking for stories, artifacts and lost civilizations. Our father co-wrote some of his tales for men's adventure magazines. Each time he returned from these dangerous excursions, he brought the raw footage he'd shot and showed it to us first. On one South American trip, he found a *coatimundi* which he named Panchito and smuggled on the plane inside his jacket. At our house the exotic pet roamed our living room, nibbling the dust jackets off books on the lowest shelves. Romaine came and spoke to my fourth-grade class, demonstrating a blow gun and poison darts used by one of the jungle tribes. (Much better show-and-tell than Boyce's tonsils in a jar.)

There were others. Some were friends from our dad's college days, science fiction and mystery writers; our family doctor who experimented with leeches (not on us) and knew about cooking rattlesnake; a motorcycle cop who taught us how to dig for arrowheads along the California coast; a museum curator who showed us through dim storerooms, spoke Native American dialects and knew sacred dances.

Any hours we spent in the company of these friends made our hearts lighter, our minds race. But it was overhearing the night-time conversations that heightened the wonder.

My brother and I were past 50 when we first spoke of the nights we would lie quietly in our rooms, pretending to sleep and fighting to stay awake in our tiny house so we could hear the grown-up talk. Our younger sister sometimes slept through these hours but we struggled to hear every word. This was when the aliens and the ghosts and the seances, the spiders and the shrunken heads, the impossible and the terrifying and the gruesome were revealed.

This was the really good stuff. So we strained and listened, letting ourselves experience how enormous and unknowable the world really was, finding in these low-voiced exchanges not something to frighten us, but something to ignite and empower. We felt that we had been let in on The Secrets, allowed to know, perhaps unintentionally, that life, rich and full, existed beyond what the eye could see.

The three of us still carry those stories and their tellers in our pockets . . . like touchstones, like arrowheads or ghost town glass, like magic beans.

Process and practice

Creating habit, changing course, all is process and process is slow. Slow is a tireless teacher.

It is now 146 days since I began a practice of wheelchair yoga, inspired by and following the book, *Sunlight Chair Yoga–Yoga for Everyone*, by Stacie Dooreck.

When I first ordered the book, I showed it to the nurse practitioner who sees me at home. A second floor apartment, very steep outside stairs and greatly diminished mobility have me, for now, playing the part of Rapunzel. The NP was enthusiastic and encouraged starting to work with the book, "*Ten minutes a week*," she suggested. For a time I resisted, claiming that I had a prior commitment to art every day, "*or so help me*." And then one day it changed, as absolutes do. And now, for more than the stated One Hundred Days, I have begun to build a practice of 35 to 40 minutes a day which equals about four hours a week and I am not the same as when I started.

A friend with whom I Skype from time to time, told me well before I reached the hundred days, that I had been "*youthified*," appeared thinner, she heard more life in my voice, more strength, she complimented my complexion and my consistence. I feel that, other than in supernatural heat, my sleep is better, my desire to overeat compulsively is diminished, and an enhanced state that I will call balance of mind has crept up on me. I am able to complete tasks in whatever increments they require, however long they take, making space for them with room for the unexpected. If I will not make a deadline, I call and reschedule. Process.

In a recent donation of books to a thrift store, I set a maximum number of grocery bags that would be included in this round of clearing. That allowed me to stop when the number was reached, knowing I could call them again for a return trip—or several. I've pictured creating a map of what I want to accomplish in nest fluffing and may go ahead and draw it. There may be "before" and "after" scenes with no life-or-death dates for completion of anything. Rather than my old way of creating needless stress for my son and me, I have become more caring of our time, our physical resources and, much as I still have pipe dreams of being turned into House Lovely by some magic hand, a very gradual, wary acceptance of who I am and how I do things has emerged.

As I am still a newbie to such a practice, I know what has been revealed, what has been altered, is only the beginning. Under life's umbrella of process is the act of surrender, over and over and over. I simply await direction. The best description I can give is that I show up every day for the series of poses and movements, complete them, and let go of everything else until the next indicated thing becomes clear, which it always does. There are days with drawing and coloring, days of sorting and sifting, days of lifting and, after a fashion, muscling things about. I remain seriously committed to a daily sharing of what I find beautiful, inspiring and encouraging on Facebook. That assignment is clear. I've gotten over the notion that such an intention is trivial, lightweight. It is part of my work and part of my joy. Beauty and love, optimism and humor are the antidotes to every pox and toxin that would knock us to our knees.

Being in touch with friends makes me happy, though I have yet to master being a timely and reliable correspondent. Always process. I trust what I do manage to send forth will be adequate, possibly welcome and not seen as falling horribly short of expectations. Process is where we learn to major in patience. Along with possibly quantifiable gifts of beginning a practice, I think I am finding those aspects of human existence which cannot be counted, which may not have any name beyond spirit. For some years now I've felt that all life is an act of faith. That feeling grows stronger. Peace and trust help diminish the deadly stress-produced chemicals that claimed me for so long.

Because I have seen so many movies based on samurai and kung fu warriors, it is a metaphor that springs easily to mind, tremendous inner strength to withstand relentless outer forces. I would like to be strong in every sense of the word, to be quiet and calm, reasonable, healthy (heaven knows!), resilient, clear and kind. I would like to be steady, firm in mind and body, not practicing juggling in the way I once did. Not teetering, no fancy footwork, yet flexible. Some of you may be familiar with one of my Rubbermoon stamps, "*Impossible Things Happen.*"

Yes, yes they do.

Interior

My own exterior and the spaces I occupy are candidates for sprucing up. Little by little I work toward a mythical day of declaring all officially spruced. The interior is a different business. I don't imagine a day of completed interior tidying. I declare myself a work in progress and leave it at that.

These thoughts were sparked by beginning, last Saturday, year two of a daily chair yoga practice. That year one is now in the record books seems a miracle or something very much like one. When we were told "one day at a time," in our best moments we hoped we could manage such seemingly small increments. Continuity is created with baby steps. That a year now passes so swiftly is a mixed blessing. That time, as I experience it, simply evaporates, often without a trace, is disturbing. Yet its quality of vanishing even as I observe it makes 365 days of committed practice more possible than I could have guessed. Next is the addition of daily art, either as work or play. There are goals and desires. I see daily work as the only reliable road.

Another interior assignment is rumination or the clearing of unhelpful thoughts, replacing them with ways of seeing that lead me away from chaos. We seem generally to have been stockpiling chaos and are now cursed with a surplus which threatens to engulf everything. If ground coffee still came in cans, I could pour mine into the empty ones as I once did bacon grease. If I still had a back yard I could bury them there. Beneath the pine and the camellia bushes, the earth was shady and damp in all four seasons. In the absence of coffee cans and a private, walled garden, I've sought other solutions.

I adhere to the belief that our capacity for change is infinite. We do what we can, with what we have, from where we are. I realize that in my younger life, and possibly still today, I have been stupid in a thousand different ways. If I could go back, there is much I would do differently. But we only know what we know when we know it, if at all. I believe that simply being kind in any and all situations will never be a bad choice for me. I know that, once spoken, harsh words cannot be unsaid.

This, this living, is all so temporary and fragile, so finite. Everything we love is really just on loan and we are wise to treat everyone and everything that matters as sacred. We befriend and, one hopes, become the better angels we seek.

I think we may be missing the good parts

CBS's *Sunday Morning* had an editorial segment on the pitfalls of multi-tasking; scientific information that it has altered the human brain, requiring (my interpretation) more and greater distraction and stimulation of busy nothingness. For one who, in my best moments, may be said to *task* this is not breaking news.

Driving and talking on the phone seems like folly on four wheels. I used to work with my color pencils as I talked on the house phone—I no longer do that, for both activities got too little of me. I am unable to turn away from a heating pan to find something in the drawer without the pan's contents boiling over. I can watch clouds—or just the sky, bare of ornament—for lengths of time that make me blush. I have evolved into the champion of my childhood picture book, *Ferdinand the Bull.* My wish is to smell the flowers, in a literal or figurative sense, and keep the agenda as simple as possible.

The first odious thing about multi-tasking is the phrase. Is it so difficult to say, "I'm having to do several things at once?" It feels like a robot language—we've programmed the glombot to multi-task . . . could it be one of the apps? Yes, I have a cell phone. Our house may have been the last in California to relinquish its analog models . . . we couldn't even get a signal in our carport. We talk, we text, and I (can't speak for anyone else) type out my complete words on the phone keypad, paying attention and sometimes hitting the wrong key, sending a message before its time and receiving "???????????????" in response.

Doing something which requires time also deserves attention, whether it is my first choice of activity or not. When our task is one which fulfills us, why would we want to diminish the pleasure by doing something less appealing at the same moment? My suspicion that we are on the brink of irreversible overload makes me protective of what cells or neuropathways or functions remain. What stresses the mind also stresses the body, which should be reason enough to reconsider.

We have been fed a lot of baloney in our lives. Multi-tasking is not a virtue; it is a way of cheapening, dulling and diluting our experiences. Please, sit down and watch the movie, do the crossword, listen to the friend who has called, or call back when you can be present. Stop what you're doing when someone comes home at the end of the day and wants your attention.

When resources are diminished, it may be all that we are able to give is our time. That may be what is needed most. One thing at a time, whether for ourselves or another. One thing at a time.

Oh, Pioneers

Each morning I, and I suspect most of us, awake to a new planet, as though we've traveled through a night made of years, suspended. In so many ways the world begins afresh every day.

What was true yesterday may no longer be so. How I felt yesterday may have pivoted, spun like the arrow on a wheel of fortune, aiming now at peace and optimism when yesterday's forecast spoke of overwhelming dither, borderline hysteria based on nothing other than my thoughts. The mercurial qualities of human emotions, beliefs and apprehensions keep me off balance more often than is comfortable. Stability is gained through plain hard work.

Gravity shifts, don't let them tell you it doesn't. What was solid beneath my feet 30 seconds ago could become quicksand due to some slight adjustment of the earth's plates or a reversal of circumstance. What we have is this moment and, if we are very lucky, the next and the next without expectation but also without fear. Try and make those pieces fit together.

I become disappointed in myself when I find I am being too critical, too judgmental of actions chosen by others. I forget what they do is mostly not my business. Any time I spend looking too hard at their questionable, often troubling antics is time I no longer have for cleaning out my own disturbingly over-filled closets.

Consistency doesn't just elude me, it avoids me, dodging behind the hibiscus when it sees me on the sidewalk. That hasn't yet stopped me from trying to find it, somehow enticing it to my uncertain embrace. It may be that not all of us are intended to be steadfast, though I can't imagine why. Reliability is such a virtue.

But then, is any of us intended to be anything other than human. Some of the variables are far beyond our control.

That each day is its own separate entity demands flexibility, improvisation. What worked on the planet we left as we fell asleep may have no value or possibility in this new location. What adjustments we make to glide or lurch through today with as little damage as possible may serve no purpose tomorrow.

It is change that is our constant, not only as a society but in our small, day-to-day lives. I envision a well-trained boxer, light of foot, quick to dodge surprising blows, ready for anything. I think, too, of ships setting forth with hope but not absolute certainty of a round planet, oceans which would eventually lead them home. We forget that we are still conquistadors, Vikings, pioneers, Lewis and Clark. We forget that, each day, we find a new path through uncharted lands, somehow traverse uncrossable waters. If we are occasionally weary of such adventure, it is fitting. We have never been here, right here, before.

Subtraction

A blog post is calling me but my blog is inaccessible without a computer. So it lands here.

For myself, I have reimagined depression and renamed it grief. Too many losses, large and less so by popular definitions, over too long and too short a time, leave us reeling. I believe I am not alone in this.

I have noticed that each fresh loss arrives with all previous losses in tow. A package deal. As I actively ponder why I feel so bewildered and shell-shocked by a new subtraction, I revisit the list, just the most recent entries. Grief is the houseguest who will not leave. Its fingers cannot be pried from the couch arm, it will not be pushed out the front door. Whatever its actual home, it has chosen to make this its permanent address. Trying to keep it from running the show, there's the challenge.

How to make peace with another death, a diagnosis, another rent increase, a dissolution, friends confronted by their realities, and me, confronted by my own.

But it matters, after a lifetime of depression, to call this angst by its true name. Grief, for all that has been taken or lost or simply eroded. For all that is gone or never was. I now use my phone's calculator function to add my daily nutritional totals. I can still compute subtraction without help.

Maintaining equilibrium, proceeding in spite of. Each day contains magic, shines with a unique light. Being *The Little Engine That Could* while acknowledging the train wreck, the truth for each of us. I was in a long-ago writing workshop with a man who could juggle. I once worked in a public arts program with a woman who knew how to walk a tightrope. An artist friend of my family could walk on his hands. Maybe seeing this all as a carnival, a circus, for which we've been hired to showcase our special, most unusual talents gives us a different, digestible context. It could be a Ray Bradbury story, a Fellini movie.

May we each keep our balance. May we be there for each other, for ourselves, on our most teetering days.

Acknowledgments

For the astonishing fact that this assortment of blog posts, written over 10 years, exists, I owe unquantifiable gratitude to three friends—Claire Beynon and Penelope Todd who first thought to bring this together for me during a difficult time, and Karen Mireau who joined the team to put it into publishable form and guide us to making it become a real book.

My admiration and gratitude for my son Lucas is almost beyond my ability to express. If we are lucky, we have champions, heroes. Lucas is one of those.

I thank all the other bloggers who read and encouraged me, whose writing inspired me, and whom I count among my friends.

The painting on the front and back cover by my brother, Mike Leadabrand, a Christmas gift, brought the perfect visual to accompany the words.

I thank Tom Oldfield for stepping up to this project graciously. His photographs capture the painting at its brilliant best.

I thank Joan Bunte, who first assigned me a "Word of the Week" blurb for her store newsletter. It was so much fun, I just kept going with it.

There are so many who have encouraged me as a writer. Some who have helped me get my foot in the door for actual jobs. These include Winifred, Jackie, Liz, Ruth, Shirley, Carl, Phil, and Jane.

Others in my life are angels, bringing light in all weather, no matter what. Thank you Claire, Dana and Ted, Melissa, Lisa, Jeanieva, Nanci, Laurie and Jay, Jean and Emmanuel, Sylvia and Cara, Andrea, Suzie, Lynne, Susan, Rebecca, and Kae Pea.

The most difficult part of this compilation is the fear of leaving anyone out. I will say that I am grateful to so many for their friendship, love, and kind words showered on me and my efforts. I am thankful for so much love in my life. Blessings, all.

About the Author

A Southern California native, Marylinn Kelly grew up in the midst of creativity, talent, and mild eccentricity.

Her mother, an artist, and her father, a writer, created an atmosphere rich in words, music, movies, art, and episodes of adventure. She acquired the skill of contemplation on frequent, often lengthy family road trips—ones that fueled her imagination.

Through her writing and her work in a variety of media, Marylinn communicates those early, wide-ranging observations of a life where things were frequently not ordinary.

To get in touch with the Author
you may follow her on Instagram:
@marylinnkelly

To get in touch with the Publisher:
KarenMireauBooks@gmail.com

For Print and Ebook orders:
www.lulu.com/shop

www.ingramcontent.com/pod-product-compliance
Lightning Source LLC
LaVergne TN
LVHW091032080826
845145LV00002B/456

* 9 7 8 1 9 6 8 8 2 2 0 7 1 *